ASTD Trainer's WorkShop Series

Negotiation
Skills
TRAINING

Lisa J. Downs

ASTD
P R E S S
Alexandria, Virginia

ASTD Press is an internationally renowned source of insightful and practical information on workplace learning and performance topics, including training basics, evaluation and return-on-investment, instructional systems development, e-learning, leadership, and career development.

Ordering information: Books published by ASTD Press can be purchased by visiting our website at store.astd.org or by calling 800.628.2783 or 703.683.8100.

Library of Congress Control Number: 2007941491

ISBN-13: 978-1-56286-536-8

ASTD Press Editorial Staff:
Director: Dean Smith
Manager, Acquisitions and Author Relations: Mark Morrow
Editorial Manager: Jacqueline Edlund-Braun
Senior Associate Editor: Tora Estep
Editorial Assistant: Gina Del Priore
Editing and Production: Aptara Inc., Falls Church, VA, www.aptaracorp.com
  Development/Production Editor: Robin C. Bonner
  Copyeditor: Ellen N. Feinstein
  Indexer: Kidd Indexing
  Proofreader: Sarah A. Bonner
Cover Design: Kristi King
Cover Illustration: ImageZoo/Images.com

Printed by Versa Press, Inc., East Peoria, Illinois, www.versapress.com

The ASTD Trainer's WorkShop Series is designed to be a practical, hands-on road map to help you quickly develop training in key business areas. Each book in the series offers all the exercises, handouts, assessments, structured experiences, and ready-to-use presentations needed to develop effective training sessions. In addition to easy-to-use icons, each book in the series includes a companion website with PowerPoint presentations and electronic copies of all supporting material featured in the book.

C o n t e n t s

◆

◆

Whether we consciously realize it or not, our lives are filled with an almost endless array of negotiations. From something as simple as deciding with family members what to have for dinner, to more complex situations, such as resolving a disagreement with a customer or coworker or working with a vendor to supply a service, being a good negotiator is a skill (and some would say an art) that can serve us well. Successful negotiation goes beyond resolving conflict. It involves a delicate balance of having our needs met while building and nurturing relationships. The better we negotiate, the greater our chances of fulfilling our needs and strengthening relationships through showing an interest in the needs of others. This also leads to the development of trust and respect.

As you can imagine, there is a great deal of information available about negotiation strategies and techniques. Some may say that the idea of a "win-win" agreement, in which both parties have their needs met, is a bit of a fantasy—that regardless of what happens, one side will need to give something up to reach an agreement. I tend to be a bit more optimistic and would suggest that it is all in how you approach the negotiation and the degree to which you are willing to truly understand the needs of your counterpart. My hope is that you are able to take the contents of this book and use it to help others learn and apply strategies and tools to improve their negotiation skills, so they are able not only to have their needs (and those of their organization) met, but also to continue to build successful personal and professional relationships.

This book is organized in a way that allows trainers to easily focus their efforts on the needs of their learners and client organizations. It provides practical exercises that walk participants through analyzing their own negotiation behaviors, learning a step-by-step process for negotiation, and practicing specific negotiation skills to use in a variety of situations. The training modules presented here challenge trainees to try strategies, with which they may be unfamiliar, in a context that encourages flexibility in a supportive learning environment. Each of your learners will negotiate in a different way; the key is to provide them with tools to adapt and improve their skills to help them experience greater success with a topic that may be uncomfortable for them.

The chapters include a number of original and adapted structured experiences and instruments developed specifically for this book. Please feel free to adjust them to meet your needs and apply them to other aspects of your learning program. Many can be used for a wide range of training topics, such as conflict management, communication skills, management skills, and training on influencing others. Some may already be familiar to you, as there are many effective foundational activities and models around negotiation that work so well that it only makes sense to include them here.

Many thanks to Mark Morrow at ASTD Press for the opportunity to write this book and for his flexibility, guidance, and encouragement during the process. I always appreciate Mark's understanding and support, and his willingness to continue to help me grow in my writing experience. Thank you, as well, to Robin Bonner and her team at Aptara Corporation for their professionalism and expertise in working through the editorial and composition processes.

Thank you to my friends, family, and learning and development colleagues with ASTD Puget Sound and beyond, who offered their support and enthusiasm during this experience. Special thanks to Aron Steven and my teammates at T-Mobile for their ongoing excitement and support for my continued adventures in publishing, and for viewing this aspect of my professional life as an asset to the organization. I consider myself lucky to work with all of you.

Finally, thank you to my husband, Chris, who is my greatest champion and a better negotiator than he may think.

Lisa J. Downs

Redmond, Washington

January 2009

◆

Introduction: How to Use This Book Effectively

What's in This Chapter?

- Practical definition of negotiation
- Discussion of common issues in teaching negotiation skills
- Explanation of how to use this workbook most effectively

What Is Negotiation?

The term *negotiation* is defined as a means to reach mutual agreement through communication. As a way to handle differences, or opposing views, with the objective of achieving your goals, negotiation involves mastery of a set of skills, such as planning, questioning, using effective nonverbal communication, brainstorming, and evaluating needs. It is often necessary for an individual to experiment with various negotiating techniques to discover a blend of strategies that works best. A willingness to discover common interests and adapt communication styles is at the core of effective negotiation.

Negotiation generally involves a five-step process: analysis, preparation, communication, proposal, and commitment. It can be an introspective process and involves a number of behaviors and tools to be most effective. Each step requires specific skills, and some people may move through the process more quickly than others. Individuals may find various aspects of negotiation to be a challenge: Assessing the style of a negotiation counterpart, selecting appropriate tactics, managing barriers to negotiation, and attending to ethical issues can be difficult. Self-awareness plays an important role in being a good negotiator. A large part of the facilitator's role in a negotiation skills workshop is to help learners recognize their strengths and weaknesses when it comes to how they typically negotiate, as well as to help them develop strategies to increase their negotiating effectiveness.

For purposes of this workbook, *negotiation* is defined as seeking agreement through dialogue.

Why This Is Important

Negotiation is a set of behaviors that may take different forms for different people. The behaviors and tools used by someone in one situation may not be the same as those used in another, and it is important to emphasize this point when you teach negotiation skills. Although an individual can learn a process to follow, as well as certain behaviors, that lead to more success as an effective negotiator, learners may not use all of the techniques provided in a workshop. They may also use strategies in different ways to improve their negotiation skills and comfort level, and this is perfectly acceptable. This book helps accelerate development and effective training delivery to prepare participants to improve their negotiation skills and interpersonal communication.

How the Book Was Developed

The author reviewed available literature on effective negotiation training and combined this knowledge with her extensive experience in teaching negotiation and conflict management skills, as well as in the design and delivery of effective, interactive training for adult learners. As a leader of numerous seminars in many aspects of interpersonal communication, the author currently serves as a workshop facilitator and coach to help others improve their personal effectiveness.

The Context of the Training

The materials and designs in this book lend themselves to a broad array of organizations, both public and private. The training materials help make participants aware of their negotiating behaviors and then develop the skills necessary to be an effective negotiator. Although the book is designed to train people for one-on-one negotiating scenarios, many of the approaches and principles also apply to small- or large-group negotiating situations with little or no adjustment.

The Content of the Training

The various aspects of negotiation, which include types, behaviors, principles, and barriers, will be new information for many learners. Some participants or organizations, however, may not consider negotiation to be a skill that requires much training; they may think that someone is either a good negotiator or a bad negotiator, and there is not much that can be done about it. This viewpoint increases the difficulty of teaching negotiation skills for some trainers.

Another related issue in some organizations is the lack of resources, particularly time, to offer training of this nature. Other training topics, initiatives, or projects may take priority over effective negotiation. To help mitigate this issue, clearly identify and communicate the desired results of the training so participants and others in the organization understand the benefits and skills taught during an effective negotiation workshop.

The training designs in this workbook are intended to address these concerns. The content modules in chapter 10 are aligned with basic knowledge required for effective negotiation and skills, particularly ways of engaging in a negotiation conversation while being aware of a negotiation counterpart's behavior.

- **Content Module 10–1: Participant Introductions.** To help create a collaborative learning environment, this module introduces participants to each other and suggests that their roles are to contribute to the learning process.

- **Content Module 10–2: Types of Negotiations.** This module explains the two most common types of negotiations and the four most common outcomes of any negotiation conversation.

- **Content Module 10–3: Negotiation Self-Assessment.** This module helps participants assess their negotiation strengths and weaknesses, and it explores how poor negotiation can negatively affect communication with others.

- **Content Module 10–4: Core Principles of Negotiation.** Negotiation principles such as BATNA (*Best Alternative To a Negotiated Agreement*), ZOPA (*Zone Of Possible Agreement*), and identification of "wants" versus "needs" are explained in this module.

- **Content Module 10–5: Steps to Negotiation.** The five-step process for effective negotiation is included in this module.

- ◆ **Content Module 10–6: Investigating Interests.** This module helps participants understand and use techniques to discover the interests of a negotiation counterpart and incorporate them into a negotiation plan.

- ◆ **Content Module 10–7: Building Trust and Relationships.** This module helps participants understand another's point of view, as well as how to ask good questions as a tool to build trust.

- ◆ **Content Module 10–8: Negotiation Tactics.** Participants have the opportunity to practice and explore the many tactics used in negotiation, as well as learn how to recognize them.

- ◆ **Content Module 10–9: Barriers to Negotiation.** This module gives participants the opportunity to identify various obstacles to negotiation situations, as well as learn how to deal with them.

- ◆ **Content Module 10–10: Ethics in Negotiation.** Although such issues are often overlooked, this module examines ethical issues in negotiation and the critical role they play.

- ◆ **Content Module 10–11: Negotiation Success Factors.** This module reviews the many factors for successful negotiation and includes a wrap-up activity to help participants focus on a negotiation success plan.

The Probable Realities of Participants

Most participants in a training course have common issues and common experiences. Although the needs-assessment process will provide specific information for a particular group of participants or for an organization, the following issues are present in many workshop situations. Awareness of these issues may help the trainer design and facilitate a training program on effective negotiation.

- ◆ **Participants may not want to be in the training workshop.** Not all attendees want to sit in class, and some consider it to be a waste of their time, particularly if the training topic is on the soft side. All or some of the participants may have been required to attend the workshop as part of a mandatory curriculum.

- ◆ **Participants may not have a clear understanding of the desired results of the training.** Lack of clarity about the benefits of attending a workshop on effective negotiation, as well as about the skills they will learn, may negatively affect learners' participation.

◆ **Participants may not have had any training on how to be a good negotiator.** Negotiation is often viewed as a naturally occurring skill. People are often told that they are good negotiators or need to be better negotiators, but they may be unclear about what that means and how to improve. It's a good sign that they are attending the workshop, but the participants may not have had any formal training on the topic prior to the program.

◆ **Some participants may not have time to practice their negotiation skills.** People often see the skills they learn in a workshop as an addition to their normal tasks and activities. In particular, some may feel that it will take more time to prepare to negotiate well and that they do not always have the additional time to do this. Although this could be the case, some participants may have trouble understanding how they can incorporate new learning into their lives.

◆ **Participants may perceive the training as a sign that they are highly deficient in negotiation skills.** Those participants for whom training is mandatory may be embarrassed, depending upon their level of negotiation skills. This perception may or may not be true. Some people view training as a remedial activity rather than one designed to enhance personal and professional effectiveness; such an attitude may affect the level of participation in training exercises.

◆ **Participants come into the training with marked differences in their skill and knowledge levels.** A single workshop may include participants from all levels in the organization's hierarchy with varying degrees of knowledge, skill, and experience. Those at the high end of the spectrum may think the workshop is not aligned with their experience level, and those at the lower level may be intimidated to be in the same training as their supervisors or senior management.

◆ **Participants may not have any clear incentive to improve their negotiation skills.** Some training attendees may not be internally motivated to develop their negotiation skills; no consequence, such as a negative score on a performance measure, may exist to encourage participation. In these situations, the trainer may face resistance to participation in workshop activities or large-group discussion.

◆ **Need to negotiate effectively may be tied to increasing customer satisfaction.** For many participants, improvement in negotiation skills may affect their relationships with their clients or customers, which in turn leads to referrals and increases in status or compensation.

◆ **Participants have received a specific directive to improve their negotiation skills.** Some participants may attend the training session to learn ways to address specific situations or issues with their negotiation skills. Although this could easily enhance the workshop, participants may attempt to steer discussion and activities toward a particular issue, which could inhibit the learning experience for others.

◆ **Participants may need to deal with competing interests during the training.** Whether they need to check voicemail, handle email, or deal with an urgent client issue, some participants may not fully attend the workshop or may attempt to multitask during the negotiation skills training. This may affect the learning environment and the effectiveness of training activities, as well as the others' workshop experiences.

How to Use This Book

The best use of this resource is to develop and conduct training sessions to improve the negotiation skills of learners. Both experienced and novice trainers will be able to use this book in a flexible manner to ensure that their sessions meet the real needs of their client organizations.

Sample training designs are included in the text, along with the materials they require. The individual content modules, structured experiences, assessments, and training instruments can also be incorporated into training already offered, or they can be mixed and matched into a variety of custom designs.

The author strongly suggests that you:

◆ Identify your target audience for effective negotiation training.

◆ Assess the learning needs of potential participants.

- Modify the enclosed designs, if necessary, or develop new ones.

- Evaluate the outcomes of the participants' training sessions to ensure their continuous improvement as trainers and of the training sessions.

This book can be a reference from which you borrow the structured experiences, instruments, assessments, and designs that fit your specific needs. A comprehensive set of steps that can help you get the most value out of this book appears at the end of this chapter under the heading "What to Do Next."

The Book's Organization

This resource contains numerous individual items that can be combined in many training designs for learners. Here are the major sets of materials:

- **Methods and effective practices** to assess the learning needs of actual or potential participants (chapter 2).

- **Evaluation methods and effective practices** for effective negotiation sessions, including assessment of the trainer and continuous improvement approaches (chapter 5).

- **Content modules** that are either ready to use or that can be modified to meet specific needs (chapter 10).

- **Assessments and training instruments** that address several vital dimensions of negotiating effectiveness (chapter 11 and online materials).

- **Structured experiences** on a variety of topics relevant to effective negotiation training (chapter 12 and online materials).

- **Microsoft Word documents** to help customize the participant manuals (online materials).

- **Microsoft PowerPoint presentations** to help trainers make presentations and give instructions (online materials).

- **Bibliography** of additional resources that can support effective negotiation training.

The goals of this book are to instruct and equip trainers with the tools to design and conduct negotiation training for learners that is highly interactive, engaging, and clearly on target.

Icons

Assessment: Appears when an agenda or learning activity includes an assessment, and it identifies each assessment presented.

Website: Indicates the online materials accompanying this workbook.

Clock: Indicates recommended timeframes for specific activities.

Discussion Questions: Points out questions you can use to explore significant aspects of the training.

Handout: Indicates handouts that you can print or copy and use to support training activities.

Key Point: Alerts you to key points that you should emphasize as part of a training activity.

PowerPoint Slide: Indicates PowerPoint presentations and slides that can be used individually. These presentations and slides are included in the online materials accompanying this workbook, and copies of the slides are included at the end of chapter 9. Instructions for using PowerPoint slides and the online materials are in the Appendix.

Structured Experience: Introduces structured experiences (participant exercises), which are included in chapter 12.

Training Instrument: Identifies specific tools, checklists, and assessments that are used before, during, and after the training workshop.

What to Do Next: Highlights recommended actions that will help you make the transition from one section of this workbook to the next, or from one specific training activity to another within a training module.

What to Do Next

◆ Study the entire contents of the book to get an overview of the resources it contains.

◆ Review the content of the online materials so that you can understand how it relates to the material in the printed book. Open the files in Microsoft Word, PowerPoint, and Adobe Acrobat Reader so you are able to determine how to make copies of the forms you will need to print and the presentations you may use to enrich the material. This step should include a careful reading of the Appendix, "How to Use the Online Materials."

◆ Study and apply the strategies outlined in chapter 2, "Assessing the Needs of Learners," to ensure that your sessions with learners are relevant and timely.

◆ When you have absorbed the information you discover in your training needs assessment, proceed to chapter 3. Design your session to meet the specific learning needs your potential participants have expressed. Carefully consider modifying the designs in this book as you formulate your plan to facilitate the learning of your client audience. You can use the sample designs in chapters 6 through 9 or modify them as your needs analysis suggests. The content modules in chapter 10 are detailed. You can plan to use them as they are or modify them. Chapters 11 and 12 contain the structured experiences, assessments, and training instruments the modules require. Because each of these is also a stand-alone item, you can easily incorporate any or all of them into your existing training designs.

◆ Prepare to facilitate your training by studying the approaches in chapter 4. Each of your sessions should improve on the previous ones, and that chapter contains tips on how you can make sure that you learn along with your trainees. You will become a highly effective facilitator; the trainees will become highly effective negotiators.

◆ Plan to evaluate each of your training sessions. Chapter 5 tells you why this is important and gives you steps to gain insight into the payoffs of your negotiation training. Outline the steps you will take to gather and analyze evaluation data, and modify your training design as a result.

Assessing the Needs of Learners

What's in This Chapter?

- Methods for needs assessment

- Tips to improve your assessment

- How to use two key assessment tools

- Guidelines for conducting successful focus groups

Assessment Steps

A training needs assessment identifies how training can meet the needs of an organization and of learners. It serves as the foundation for a successful training program and supports employee performance with the ultimate goal of adding value to meet an organization's business needs. These are the common steps to conduct a needs assessment:

- **Identify the business needs of the organization and determine its culture.** A needs assessment will help gauge whether a negotiation skills workshop is indeed a solution or whether there is some other underlying performance issue present in the organization. Sometimes, an organization may think training will cure all ills, and if so, an assessment will reveal this information. Ask such questions as: Which business strategies would an effective negotiation training support? Which business problems could negotiation skills training help solve? Which data exists that may provide insight into this business need? Which measures will be used to determine whether the training has had an effect on the business?

- **Identify the performance and learner needs.** It's important to know which behaviors need to change to determine whether effective negotiation training is the appropriate solution. Data regarding potential learners' current and required performance, as well as their current and required skill and knowledge levels, will be helpful during this step in the needs-assessment process. Ask such questions as: What do learners need to stop, or to start doing differently? What are the learners' current levels of achievement with regard to being good negotiators, and what should they be? What knowledge and skills should employees learn to be effective negotiators? What are the learning styles of potential participants?

- **Analyze the data.** The data collected will reveal whether an effective negotiation skills workshop should be recommended, and if so, who should be in the training. Look at any gaps in performance, knowledge, and skills, and then determine the best candidates for the training based on the needs of the learners and the organization.

- **Deliver recommendations.** Present the findings of the assessment, including training and nontraining recommendations (processes and procedures, environment, and accountability). Share information regarding how the success of effective negotiation training will be measured, how the training will be designed and delivered, and how the program will be evaluated.

The following methods and tools can help you complete the assessment process.

Methods

Many strategies determine what potential training participants need to learn. Some are more time consuming than others, but here are five that are used frequently:

- **Existing data.** This can include benchmarking reports, performance appraisals, strategic plans, competency models, financial reports, job descriptions, mission statements, and annual reports. The advantage of this method is that the information is readily accessible from the organization and provides hard, reliable data and measures. Because this information is typically gathered for purposes other than training, it is necessary to make inferences from it to determine whether training issues are present.

◆ **Surveys.** Participants answer a series of focused questions, typically by a deadline; results are easy to tally and analyze. This method is usually an inexpensive way for respondents to provide information quickly and easily, either via an electronic tool or a paper-and-pencil questionnaire. It is important, however, to word the questions carefully so you get the desired data and the questions mean the same thing to each respondent.

◆ **Interviews.** Interviews are one-on-one discussions, either face-to-face or over the phone, to gather data about individual learner and business needs. Plan interview questions ahead, record the session (with the interviewee's permission), and take notes. Although this is a time-consuming method, it can provide great detail and draw out information that is difficult to obtain from a survey. The interviewer must objectively record responses and not add his or her interpretation to what is said.

◆ **Focus groups.** A facilitator conducts a group interview, which can provide information about learners' skill and performance levels, the work environment, culture, and perceptions of potential training participants. An advantage to this data-collection method is that all participants can hear and build on each others' ideas. It can also be time consuming, and it may be beneficial to have more than one facilitator conduct a focus group session.

◆ **Observation.** The observer visits the organization to watch learners do their jobs, then records information regarding such items as behavior patterns, task performance, interactions with others, and use of time. Although this method is helpful to assess training needs and skill levels for individual learners, the observer cannot typically assess mental processes. Individuals may also behave differently around an observer than they would under normal circumstances.

Assessment Tips

Assessing the needs of learners should be carried out in a respectful, thoughtful way. Here are some tips that may help:

◆ **Gather the data that will provide an accurate and thorough assessment.** Discuss with the client what will be involved in conducting a needs assessment and the approach taken to gain buy-in.

Be sure to collect the data that will address the needs of both the learners and the organization regarding negotiation skills training, and go to the source(s) that will best be able to provide accurate, pertinent information.

◆ **Focus only on the training and nontraining needs you can provide.** A needs assessment can be a reflection of your competency, so be sure that you are able to deliver on all solutions that arise from assessment results, whether they include negotiation skills training, coaching, or fixing a breakdown in a process. Trainers need to be competent in a variety of learning and performance areas to conduct a thorough needs assessment for an organization. It is also in the best interests of the client to offer more than just a workshop as a possible solution to a performance or business issue.

◆ **Involve learners directly.** Ask learners about their needs through an interview, survey, or other assessment method; this is a simple way to gather important data and gain buy-in from potential training participants. Information about preferred learning styles, previous experience with negotiation skills training, skill levels, and what they would like to learn in an effective negotiation workshop will enhance the design and delivery of the training, as well as signal to the learners that they directly influence the content and activities in a training session.

◆ **Use a variety of data-collection methods.** Use two or three methods to ensure that the correct solution will become apparent and that the needs of the clients and learners will be met. This also helps avoid analysis paralysis and the possibility of getting bogged down by too many tools and too much information. Additionally, using different methods will help maintain reliability and objectivity throughout the needs-assessment process.

◆ **Present information free of trainer jargon.** Make an effort to address decision makers in language that is familiar to them rather than trainer or performance improvement jargon that may confuse or alienate them. As with other professions, the field of learning and development contains its own acronyms, as well as language that those outside the discipline may not understand. Stick to a discussion of success, impact on business issues, strategy, and learner needs.

Two Key Resources

Chapter 11 of this workbook contains two useful tools that trainers can use to assess the developmental needs of learners. Adapt either or both according to the client's requirements.

- ◆ **Assessment 11–1: Learning Needs-Assessment Sheet.** This tool follows the steps in conducting a needs assessment and is designed to help you record information obtained by using the interview method of data collection. Adapt this form as needed. The Microsoft Word file is included in the online materials that accompany this workbook.

- ◆ **Assessment 11–2: Negotiation Self-Assessment.** Use this assessment as either a training tool or prework for an effective negotiation training session. You may also adapt the instrument for 360-degree assessments. Edit the Word file in the online materials that accompany this workbook.

Using Focus Groups in Training Needs Assessment

Because conducting a focus group takes additional planning and can be more complex to facilitate than the other data-collection methods, what follows is some detailed information that may help you conduct a successful focus group session. A focus group is an efficient way to gather data on the learners' needs for a negotiation skills training session. It is best to have at least two facilitators conduct the focus group: one to lead the session and keep the group on track, and the other to record the information from the session. The facilitators may want to alternate the roles of facilitator and recorder, depending on the length of the session and the strengths of the facilitators. It is important to have an agenda for the session and monitor the flow of conversation, because participants may have a tendency to go off on tangents or complain about a variety of subjects. It is also difficult to capture information when participants speak quickly, so it may be best to use audio or other equipment to record the conversation.

Here is a step-by-step process you can adapt to prepare for and conduct effective focus group sessions to assess the needs of learners:

- ◆ Determine the audience for negotiation skills training, and collect the contact information for each person.

◆ Schedule, well in advance, one or two focus group sessions in private, easily accessible facilities. Allow at least an hour for each session.

◆ Invite the members of the target audience to attend one or more focus groups to discuss what they would like to gain from negotiation skills training, how improved negotiation could benefit communication in the organization, and the negotiation challenges they face. Limit the group size to five or seven members to encourage participants to speak freely and to record the conversation efficiently.

◆ Print sufficient copies of **Assessment 11–3: Needs-Assessment Discussion Form** in chapter 11, and bring along extra supplies (such as pens, pencils, and notepads) for the participants.

◆ As the focus group begins, greet and welcome each person. Introduce yourself and ask participants to introduce themselves by sharing the following information. You may want to write this list on a flipchart or whiteboard:

  ◆ Name

  ◆ Job title

  ◆ Length of service at the organization

  ◆ How would they currently rate themselves as a negotiator on a scale from 1 to 10?

  ◆ What is their biggest challenge when it comes to negotiation?

◆ Share with the participants the purpose of the needs assessment, how the data will be used, and why you were chosen to conduct the assessment. Ask their permission to record the focus group session.

◆ Hand out copies of **Assessment 11–3: Needs-Assessment Discussion Form,** and ask the participants to complete it candidly. Be sure they do not put their names on the forms, and explain that you will collect the sheets after the session.

◆ Ask the participants if they need more time, and when ready, explain that they can still make changes on the form during the discussion if they wish.

◆ Ask each person in the room the first question on the form. Be sure that you understand what each person says, and don't be afraid to ask for clarification, examples, or probe for specifics. It is also a good idea to paraphrase responses for the other members of the group. Encourage participants to share what they have in common in response to the question.

◆ Facilitate the group's discussion through the remaining questions on the form. Start with a different participant each time, and intervene when necessary if one group member starts to dominate the discussion.

◆ Summarize the common themes and ideas that came out of the discussion with the participants, and verify the accuracy of what was said.

◆ Collect the participants' discussion forms, and remind them that the information will be used to help determine the content and activities for effective negotiation training that they will be invited to attend. If the training has been scheduled, share this information with the participants.

◆ Thank the focus group members for their participation.

What to Do Next

◆ Follow the Assessment Steps outlined at the beginning of the chapter to determine how you will go about conducting a needs assessment for your training.

◆ Decide the most effective method(s) to use for your needs assessment to gather pertinent data from key stakeholders.

◆ Determine who will need to be involved in the assessment process and arrange any necessary interviews or focus group sessions.

◆ Choose the available assessment tools you will use to help you carry out your needs assessment.

◆

Designing Interactive Training

- ◆ Basic principles of adult learning

- ◆ Ideas for creating successful training sessions

- ◆ Training design tips

Principles of Design in Adult Learning

Good design is the essence of effective negotiation training, and it is a critical part of meeting the needs of learners and the client organization. Careful thought about the readiness, learning styles, and training needs of potential workshop participants will help to create an effective sequence of events to ensure that people will learn what is required in the allotted timeframe. The facilitator must have a structured plan to help learners develop the knowledge, skills, techniques, and attitudes necessary for success. A solid training design will make the trainer more comfortable and better able to deliver an effective program that capitalizes on the facilitator's strengths and abilities as it addresses the participants' needs.

Malcolm Knowles (1998) has long been considered the father of adult learning and was the first to popularize the term *andragogy* to refer to the science of teaching adults. As a result of his thorough research about the way in which adults learn, he identified several assumptions about adult learning that affect how to design training. Here is a list of those principles and the implications for negotiation skills training design:

- ◆ **Adults need to know why they must learn something before they learn it.** It is therefore the facilitator's responsibility to explain why the learning is of value and how the training will help the participants improve their negotiation skills.

◆ **Adults need to feel that others consider them to be able to make their own decisions and direct their own lives.** They may fear that training will be similar to their school experiences and thus resist participation. Trainers must create learning experiences that help adults make the transition from dependent to independent learners by providing them with useful strategies and tools.

◆ **The richest resources for adult learning are in the learners themselves.** All adults have unique experiences to share, as well as varied backgrounds, motivations, learning styles, interests, and needs. It will be most effective for the facilitator to use the participants' experiences with negotiation and communication during the training session.

◆ **Learning must be authentic, as adults are ready to learn to cope with real-life situations.** It is also important that the learning coincide with a participant's development and be appropriate for the learner's skill and knowledge levels. To ensure that the training meets the needs of all learners, facilitators can use a variety of structured experiences and can share information that directly addresses negotiation and interpersonal communication issues.

◆ **Adults are motivated to learn if they believe that the training will help them on the job and in their relationships.** The most effective training helps individuals perform tasks and handle problems that they confront in their everyday lives. Participants in an effective negotiation training session should be allowed to influence the learning approach. Facilitators should use interactive training methods that focus on how participants can apply the learning and change their behavior.

◆ **Adults are strongly motivated by internal pressures: quality-of-life issues, job satisfaction, or respect in the workplace.** Each person's type and level of motivation is different, so the trainer must identify those motivators and decide the best way to incorporate them into the training, which can be challenging.

Adult learners are goal-oriented with little time and a finite capacity to absorb information. Limit lecture time for delivering information to allow a free

Figure 3.1 Adult Learning in Practice

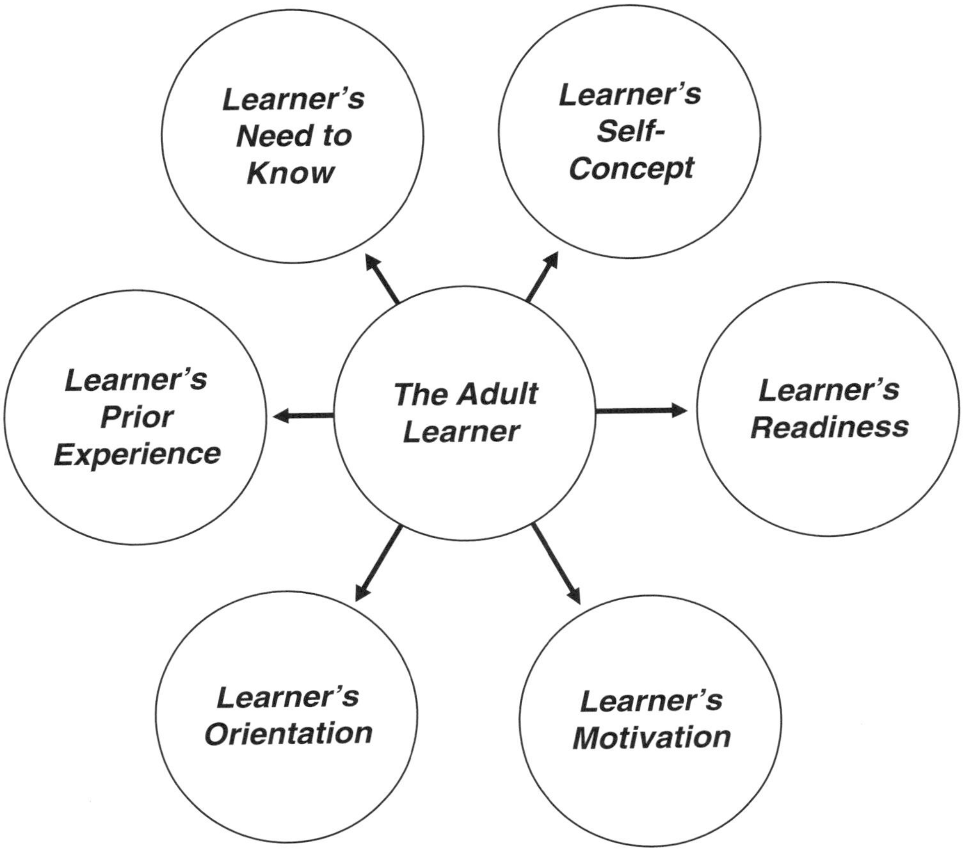

Source: Knowles, Malcolm S., Elwood F. Holton III, and Richard A. Swanson. *The Adult Learner* (5th edition). Houston: Gulf Publishing Company, 1998.

exchange of ideas, and vary the presentation. This will also provide an engaging environment and ensure that different learning styles are considered. Give participants frequent breaks during a lengthy training session so they have opportunities to attend to their needs and get a mental break.

Figure 3.1 is a visual representation of Malcolm Knowles's elements of the adult learning model.

A Note on Training Language

The information about adult learning principles and their implications for designing effective negotiation training should make it clear that training is not teaching. Facilitators should not use language associated with education.

For each word below, facilitators should substitute the training language in parentheses:

- ◆ Course (training session)

- ◆ Instructor (facilitator)

- ◆ Evaluation (assessment)

- ◆ Classroom (training room, facility, or venue)

- ◆ Textbook (participant manual or guide)

 The organizational learning experience differs greatly from most academic experiences and is more targeted and practical. Many people have negative memories of their formal schooling, so trainers should be careful to avoid such reminders when they design training.

Using the Sample Designs in This Book

If you study the sample designs in chapters 6 through 9 and the content modules in chapter 10, you will discover a number of effective practices in designing interactive training for successful negotiation. Here are the major generalizations you may make in reviewing this material:

- ◆ **Break up the training into segments.** Determine the chunks of time you have, such as a half day or a full day.

- ◆ **Break each major segment into smaller chunks.** Design each chunk so it has a beginning, middle, and end, and then structure the length of each segment according to the time required for each activity. Be sure to consider participant breaks, time to get organized, and time for the facilitator to refresh himself or herself.

- ◆ **Anticipate which training activities may take more or less time than expected.** It is always better to plan too many activities than not enough, but you may need to adjust the timing of structured experiences depending on the participation level of the learners. If an activity takes more or less time than anticipated, prepare to adjust the length of your remaining activities or insert another activity on the spot.

- ◆ **Make a seamless transition from one training activity to the next.** Create transition statements to help learners see the connection between activities, as well as how each module relates to the next, so the training does not feel segmented. One example may be, "Preparing is one step in the negotiation process. Let's take a look at another . . ." The relationships between segments may be obvious to the training designer, but meaningful transition statements will help point out these connections to the participants.

◆ **Allow plenty of time for activity debriefings.** The debriefing discussions after each activity are crucial for the participants to commit to change their behavior and apply what they have learned. They also help clarify information and are an effective way to determine whether the activity has been effective.

◆ **Create a detailed action plan for each session.** The sample action plans in this workbook provide models for you to consider. Sometimes the training design includes activities for the facilitator and participants to do after the formal session.

◆ **Share the desired results for the training with the participants.** Present an overview of the desired outcomes for the training. Refer to these outcomes throughout the session as you transition between segments and activities so learners see how the pieces fit together. This should be limited to three outcomes to be most effective.

◆ **Consider offering a follow-up session for participants.** Depending on the participants' and client organization's commitment and needs, plan a refresher session about a month or two after the training. During this meeting, you can facilitate a discussion of what worked well for the participants, what is still challenging for them, and what additional training sessions they would like to attend.

Tips for Designing Effective Training

When designing a training session, developers use a structured process to ensure that the training is effective. This work is both an art and a science, and it reflects the designer's approach to adult learning.

A common process used for training design is represented by the acronym ADDIE, which represents each of the five steps in the process: *a*nalysis, *d*esign, *d*evelopment, *i*mplementation, and *e*valuation. Here is an explanation of this method:

◆ **Analysis.** Conduct a thorough needs assessment of the client organization and its learners (see chapter 2) to determine what the training issues are and what the desired results of the learning should be.

- ◆ **Design.** Decide how to present the training content to address the learners' needs according to results of your needs assessment and adult learning principles. Determine the sequencing of the training segments and structured activities during this step.

- ◆ **Development.** Create training materials, such as PowerPoint presentations, handouts, participant manuals, and instructions for activities. This workbook provides the materials you will need to conduct effective negotiation training sessions, so it may not be necessary to spend much time on this step of the process.

- ◆ **Implementation.** Schedule the training session and handle any logistical details (book the facility, arrange catering, and make sure the materials and any necessary equipment are at the session). The facilitator must also market the training to potential participants and make any necessary changes to the content and materials.

- ◆ **Evaluation.** Assess whether the training has achieved the desired results and met the learners' needs. The different levels of evaluation are explained in more detail in chapter 5.

Because people usually remember the first and last things you say and do, pay attention to the beginning and ending activities when you design training. It's true that first impressions are important and it can be difficult to recover from a poor start, so be sure to set yourself up for success. A strong ending will leave the participants feeling confident, informed, and excited to put what they have learned into practice. Emphasize a plan of action at the end of the session.

Anticipate various problems that may occur, such as fire alarm interruptions, power outages, equipment failures, and domineering or difficult participants. A backup plan will help the training session go smoothly and will minimize stress for the facilitator.

It may also be beneficial to solicit feedback about your training design from colleagues beforehand to gauge the flow of the session and the appropriateness of activities. Ask one or more observers to sit in on a training session to help provide information on what may need to be changed and how the training can be most effective.

Ultimately, the training should be beneficial for the participants, the client organization, and the facilitator. To achieve this, the facilitator must have solid information about learning needs, as well as use resources carefully and to the fullest extent possible.

What to Do Next

- ◆ Determine how you will incorporate the principles of adult learning into your training sessions.

- ◆ Follow the suggestions for using the sample designs in this book, as outlined in this chapter.

- ◆ Use the ADDIE model for instructional design to help you select training content in line with your needs assessment data and develop an effective workshop.

- ◆ Solicit feedback from others about your training design and planned workshop activities.

◆

Facilitating Negotiation Skills Training

What's in This Chapter?

- ◆ Definition of the facilitator role
- ◆ Strategies for engaging adult learners
- ◆ Techniques for capturing and holding trainees' attention
- ◆ Tips to create a learning environment

The Role of the Facilitator

Facilitating training effectively combines the roles of event planner, public speaker, counselor, and entertainer.

- ◆ **Event Planner.** The effective delivery of a training program requires careful coordination regarding facilities, equipment, materials, and participants. Contingency arrangements must be made for times when things don't go according to plan. Large training departments may provide administrative help with logistics planning, but when participants arrive, it's the facilitator's responsibility to make sure everything is running smoothly. In larger groups, facilitation also involves crowd control. A big part of creating a productive learning environment includes making sure the participants are back from breaks on time and are refocused.

- ◆ **Public Speaker.** When you are the facilitator, the spotlight is on you. The participants depend on you for behavioral cues, and your physical presence and speaking style set the tone for the program. You need to know your material so you can convey it to others. Anything can happen in interactive design, so you must also be able to think and react quickly.

♦ **Counselor.** A facilitator's most important skill is the ability to focus on the participants' verbal comments and physical cues, as well as to understand their concerns and questions. Listening intently for an extended period of time can be mentally exhausting, so be well rested and prepared. This emphasis on the listening role is perhaps the most critical difference between facilitators and the teachers most of us experienced as students.

♦ **Entertainer.** Few of us are good stand-up comedians, and we shouldn't try to be. Nevertheless, participants feed on the energy of the facilitator. A low-energy, soft-spoken, unanimated facilitator will create a low-energy program with little participant interaction. An engaging facilitator uses humor, interesting personal stories, sincere interest in the participants and subject matter, and—most important—high energy.

Although planning, effective speaking, listening, and demonstrating high energy increase the effectiveness of a facilitator, it is also important to be yourself. Emphasize your strengths and downplay skills or behaviors with which you are less comfortable. Don't try to be someone you're not. Use the materials in this book to design a training program well suited to your skills and personality.

What Is a Facilitator?

There can be confusion within the training and development field about the terminology used. Here are some useful distinctions:

♦ **Facilitator.** From the French word "facile," which means "easy," facilitation is the art and science of assisting learners in experiencing content. The role of the facilitator is to facilitate learning for the group. Because it is the subject of this chapter, the facilitator's role will soon become clearer. Facilitation typically occurs in organizational meetings and training sessions.

♦ **Educator.** This person teaches, or disseminates, knowledge and understanding to students or pupils. The educator, or teacher, operates in classroom and laboratory settings, leading students from a position of authority and superior knowledge. In training and development terms, many educators play the role of subject matter expert.

♦ **Trainer.** This role centers on helping trainees become competent in the areas in which they work. The focal points are specific job-task knowledge, skills, and effective practices. Trainers typically operate in training rooms with groups of trainees.

- ◆ **Counselor.** Requiring specialized education and training, a counselor works in an official capacity to provide private, confidential assistance to employees with personal problems. Obviously, a facilitator may address some personal and confidential issues with employees, but the facilitator will refer him or her to a professional counselor when warranted.

- ◆ **Consultant.** With special emphasis on working with employees in a partnership arrangement, consultants help clients analyze situations that need attention, explore and evaluate options, and commit to action plans. Two basic types of consultants exist: expert and process. Experts give clients advice, but process-oriented consultants help clients learn how to improve work processes, including interpersonal ones.

The facilitator, then, works with learners in a way that helps them be open to new learning and makes the process easy. The role requires the facilitator to set up activities that foster learning through hands-on experience and interaction. A common phrase used to define the facilitator's role is "to be the guide on the side and not the sage on the stage." Major aspects of excellence in facilitation include setting up proper experiential (participative) learning activities or exercises, as well as leading discussions of the results, referred to as debriefing. The structured experiences in chapter 12 contain instructions to facilitate debriefings. It's important to devote as much time to debriefing the exercises as to conducting them so participants will understand how to apply the training content to their real-life experiences.

Engaging Adult Learners

When you consider principles of adult learning (see chapter 3), include a variety of activities in effective negotiation training that will engage the learners and encourage their participation. Although it is often necessary to convey information through lecture, for example, by going through PowerPoint slides, a facilitator should spend no more than 15–20 minutes at a time on this type of presentation. The remainder of the time in each training module should focus on leading discussions, facilitating exercises, and otherwise engaging learners to make them active participants in the session.

Mixing the training methods used in a workshop provides variety for the facilitator and the learners; at the same time, it creates excellent opportunities for trainees to share their experiences, crystallize key concepts, and develop a plan of action for applying the content of the training to their everyday lives. Here are some common training methods that lead to participative learning:

- **Large-group discussion.** The facilitator poses questions to the full group of trainees; individual learners then respond to the questions in front of everyone, and others have the opportunity to add their ideas to the discussion. Each debriefing portion of the structured experiences in chapter 12 is meant to be a large-group discussion.

- **Small-group exercises.** Participants are divided into small groups (either by forming their own groups, numbering off, or a method chosen by the facilitator), in which they can have a discussion, a hands-on activity, a brainstorming session, or a problem-solving experience. Small groups usually have a time limit in which to complete their assignment, and one or more members of each group report to the full group of trainees on what the group talked about, created, or decided.

- **Case studies.** Here, learners are provided with detailed information about a real-life situation, including all circumstances, issues, and actions of people related to the case study. Participants, working either individually or in small groups, must analyze the case study, discuss, and share what was done well, what mistakes may have been made, and the implications for the topic at hand.

- **Role playing.** Some adult learners may hear the words "role play" and want to run for the nearest exit. Role playing, however, is a very effective way for participants to practice new skills, particularly for interpersonal communication, in a safe environment. Two or more trainees spontaneously dramatize a situation that relates to a problem. Each participant acts out a role as he or she feels it would be portrayed in real life. After the other learners observe the performance, a debriefing discussion is usually held to talk about the role play and its implications. Although some role plays are conducted in front of the large group and others are done in small groups, everyone watches the debriefing portion. The facilitator needs to be sensitive to the different learners' personalities when conducting a large-group role play, because some may be uncomfortable performing in front of more than a handful of people.

- **Simulations.** A simulation is an abstract representation of a real-life situation that requires learners to solve complex problems. The facilitator creates aspects of the situation that are close to reality, and the learner must perform manipulations, respond, and take action to correct problems or maintain a certain status. Many simulations are computer controlled, such as a flight simulator for airplane pilot training. After the training, the facilitator debriefs the learners and evaluates the results of the simulation.

◆ **Games.** A game is a formalized simulation activity. Two or more participants or teams compete with each other to meet a set of objectives that relate to a training topic. Set rules and procedures for the game include information that requires decision-making and follow-up actions. Typically, the facilitator handles the scoring and may give small trinkets as prizes for the winning participants or teams. Games can be played in small or large groups.

To engage adult learners and ensure that learning is participative, it is important to use a variety of training methods. Equally important, the facilitator should capture and hold the participants' attention. Part of the facilitator's role is to guard against boredom; here are some techniques for keeping the learners interested:

◆ Open with an introductory exercise that captures learners' attention and gets them engaged within the first 15 minutes of the training session. This helps set the tone and communicates to the participants that you value and encourage their involvement.

◆ Vary your rate of speech, volume, movement, facial expressions, and gestures. Although it is best to maintain a good volume to be easily heard and avoid distracting gestures and mannerisms, these subtle techniques can coordinate with what learners should attend to during the training.

◆ Break up explanations of key concepts with videos, demonstrations, examples, or readings from articles or books. This helps create memorable experiences for the participants and keeps things lively and interesting.

◆ Use appropriate and relevant humor, shock, suspense, or surprise. Share something unexpected, a funny anecdote, a startling statistic, or an applicable comic strip to engage learners and encourage discussion. These techniques provide good opportunities for trainees to identify with the content and explore different ideas.

Use Table 4–1 as a guide to help you decide which training methods to use and how to engage learners so their training experience is as participative and effective as possible.

Table 4–1

Selecting Instructional Methods and Tools

Choosing Training Methods

For each module, determine which of the following instructional methods you will use:

❑ Large-group discussions

❑ Small-group exercises

❑ Case studies

❑ Role plays

❑ Simulations

❑ Games

❑ Lectures

Checking Training Design

For each module, make sure that you:

❑ Identify the learning objectives

❑ Anticipate questions the participants may ask and formulate responses

❑ Include enough exercises for learners to demonstrate knowledge and share past experiences

❑ Provide correct responses (if applicable) and anticipate errors for each activity

❑ Include activities that enable learners to share how they will apply content to their work

❑ Allow sufficient time for debriefing discussions after exercises

Logistics and Equipment

Check to be sure you have:

❑ Secured and tested necessary equipment to conduct the training

❑ Produced ample copies of participant materials, assessments, and tools

❑ Saved a back-up copy of your PowerPoint presentation

❑ Secured (if applicable) and visited the training facility to assess the environment

Table 4–1, continued
Selecting Instructional Methods and Tools

Other Issues to Consider

Have you provided an introductory activity that captures the attention of the learners within the first 15 minutes of the training?

❑ Yes   ❑ No

Do you have a plan for minimizing distractions during the training and communicating this to the participants?

❑ Yes   ❑ No

Have you practiced presenting the PowerPoint slides and conducting the activities in your training session?

❑ Yes   ❑ No

Do you have a plan for how you will vary your actions and create memorable experiences for the learners during the training?

❑ Yes   ❑ No

Adapted from: Carliner, Saul. *Training Design Basics*. Alexandria, VA: ASTD, 2003.

Creating the Learning Environment

Creating a positive learning environment is a critical factor in making learning easy. The facilitator should seek to create four conditions to maximize learning:

- **Confidentiality.** The first step is to admit ignorance. Some trainees may fear the repercussions of showing their weaknesses. To alleviate these concerns, assure the participants that the sole purpose of the training is to build their negotiation and communication skills, and that no evaluations will take place. If discussions and events during the training program remain confidential between the participants and facilitators, this will help create a safe, risk-free environment.

- **Freedom from distractions.** Work and personal demands cannot be ignored during training, but they should be minimized as a courtesy to others; this will help each participant benefit from the training to the fullest extent possible. Ask that cell phones, personal digital assistants, and pagers be turned off or set to inaudible alerts. Select a training site away from the workplace to help greatly reduce distractions. Acknowledge that participants don't have time to be away from work but, inasmuch as they are, ask them to immerse themselves in the learning experience to get the most value from their training. Remind them also that they will have plenty of opportunities to check messages during breaks.

◆ **Participants are responsible for their own learning.** Experiential (participative) learning requires that trainees be actively engaged and committed to learning. The facilitator can only create the opportunity to learn; he or she cannot force anyone to learn. If a participant leaves a well-designed training session (which use of this book guarantees!) saying, "I learned nothing," then that statement reflects on the participant more than on the facilitator. The facilitator's role is to create a learning environment in which participants are challenged, intrigued, and able to explore and address their own developmental needs. It is the participants' responsibility to respond to the learning environment and, if necessary, to inform the facilitator if the environment does not meet their needs.

◆ **All participants are learning partners.** Each participant brings some relevant knowledge to the training program. A successful training session will tap into each participant's knowledge as information is discussed and shared. Encourage all participants to accept responsibility for helping others learn.

What to Do Next

◆ **Plan.** Make sure you are prepared to use all of the elements of your design effectively. Plan to maximize the appropriateness of your facilitation style. What will work in your approach to training? What skills do you want to sharpen as you facilitate this training? How will you obtain coaching and feedback on these skills?

◆ **Practice.** Go through the training materials in your design carefully. Be prepared to respond to trainees' questions that the materials and activities might generate. Present the PowerPoint slide shows to a friend or colleague to become more comfortable with the points you want to make.

◆ **Recruit co-facilitators.** You and your trainees can benefit from having co-facilitators, but it can be confusing and excessive to have more than two at once. The active involvement of an experienced manager or executive as co-facilitator can greatly add to the legitimacy of your training; however, you may need to coach the person to play the role of trainer. Subject matter experts, such as a well-known motivator or teacher, can also add depth and credibility to the delivery of your training. You will need to coach each of the subject matter experts before and after the session for maximum effectiveness and minimal surprises.

◆ **Prepare all needed materials and test your equipment.** Using the online materials that accompany this book, print enough copies of the assessments and training instruments needed in your design. Set up your computer to project the PowerPoint slide shows and rehearse the ones that are necessary for your design.

Evaluating and Improving Negotiation Skills Training

- Overview of a classic training evaluation model

- How to use included instruments for your own training evaluation

- Tips on interpreting and making use of evaluation results

- Steps to successful evaluation

Why Bother?

Evaluating training can be extremely beneficial to both the trainer and the organization. Without an evaluation, you are essentially flying blind; you don't know whether the training is effective, whether participants learn anything during the training, or whether training has a positive effect on the organization.

Here are three motivations for, and benefits of, evaluating the negotiation skills training that you design and deliver:

1. The training outcomes should be aligned with the learning needs that you assessed earlier. In other words, did the training meet the needs that the learners in the organization had at the time?

2. You can justify the continuation of investing in negotiation skills and other training you provide if you can demonstrate that it is on target.

   - Did the learners like the training?

   - Did they learn the content?

◆ Did they use the content?

◆ Did it positively affect the organization's results?

3. Use a scientific approach to improve the design and delivery of the training you provide; then you can demonstrate value to the organization by linking data to business decisions. A thorough evaluation of negotiation skills training ensures that real information drives the continuous improvement of your training—not just general impressions or anecdotes. The evaluation also conveys the message that you are serious about results, and it demonstrates your business acumen.

The Classic Levels of Training Evaluation

Donald Kirkpatrick (2006) developed a well-known model for training evaluation that consists of four levels; this model guides much of the practice of measuring training outcomes in the learning and development field. The levels are graduated, from those that are relatively easy to measure to the more complex:

◆ **Level 1—Reaction:** Measure the reaction of participants to the training. Although positive reactions may not ensure that learning takes place, negative reactions can certainly affect the likelihood of learning, as well as whether the training will be offered again in the future.

◆ **Level 2—Learning:** Measure the extent to which learning objectives have been achieved. Has knowledge increased? Have skills improved or attitudes changed as a result of the training?

◆ **Level 3—Behavior:** Measure the extent to which participants changed their behavior in the organization because they attended the training.

◆ **Level 4—Results:** Measure the organizational results from behavioral changes that were achieved because participants attended the training.

The least powerful, but most common, evaluation method is at the first level. Brief reaction surveys, commonly called Smile Sheets, usually use Likert scales to measure the effectiveness of the training content and delivery, and they include space to write comments. The questions are often about value and participant enjoyment of the training. Smile Sheets indicate immediate reactions of participants, but they may have no correlation to actual learning. An entertaining facilitator, comfortable learning environment, and good food can produce positive survey results, but it may not affect application of learning and behavior change. Some participants also follow the old adage, "If you can't say anything nice, don't say anything at all." They either give high scores that don't reflect their real reactions, or they don't complete the evaluation. The participants may want to leave the training facility and beat rush-hour traffic more than they want to provide helpful feedback.

Organizations often use Smile Sheets because they are easy to administer and can provide some value. As mentioned earlier, positive scores may not be indicative of effective training, but negative evaluations are a strong indication that the training is ineffective. Also, open-ended questions that allow participants to provide comments on the training can offer important, useful feedback.

In effect, because the four evaluation levels are ranked according to complexity, they are also ranked according to decreasing use. More organizations therefore use Smile Sheets to evaluate training rather than attempt to measure learning and impact at the other three levels. Some may track learning by conducting pretests and posttests to assess skill level, but this may be limited to information technology training subjects in many organizations. Fewer track behavior changes, and still fewer try to measure business results or return-on-investment for learning programs, which is a difficult task. The author strongly recommends that trainers take whatever steps necessary to evaluate their sessions more thoroughly. If training is to be considered a key business activity, trainers must be accountable for the value they claim to add to the organization and the effect on results.

Instruments for Evaluation in This Workbook

Chapter 11 of this workbook includes four instruments that lend themselves to applications of evaluating training. Some can also be used in training designs.

- ◆ **Assessment 11–2: Negotiation Self-Assessment.** This tool calls for negotiation skills training participants to analyze their strengths and developmental needs. The instrument can be used as prework for an initial training module, as well as a repeat measure either at the end of the session or sometime afterward.

- ◆ **Assessment 11–4: Facilitator Competencies.** This form helps establish learning priorities for your own development as a workshop facilitator. It can be used as a self-assessment or as a follow-up questionnaire to solicit feedback from trainees after a session or at a later time.

◆ **Assessment 11–5: Negotiation Skills Follow-Up Assessment.** Distribute this questionnaire some time after the end of the negotiation skills training. Targeting Level 3 of Kirkpatrick's training evaluation model, it can be used in follow-up reunions of trainees or as a survey. The questionnaire can also include ratings from colleagues or supervisors in the participants' work environments.

◆ **Assessment 11–6: Training Evaluation.** Use this form to conduct a Level 1 Smile Sheet evaluation. It allows training participants to provide reaction feedback for the workshop and the facilitator.

Of course, trainers are not limited to use of these four instruments. It is important to decide upon systematic evaluation and to conduct it routinely. In this way, you build up an understanding of what works best with your trainees and communicate your value to the client organization.

Improving Negotiation Skills Training

For many organizations, the concept of continuous improvement is of critical importance. As a training professional, it is in your best interest to demonstrate your attention to detail, as well as how you achieve the desired results. Be proactive to set yourself up for success; this will enable you to meet the needs of the organization and its learners in the best way possible. Applied to negotiation skills training, commitment to continuous improvement means you:

◆ Specify the steps you are taking.

◆ Analyze the logic of the sequence.

◆ Look carefully at the effectiveness of each step.

◆ Make changes that offer chances to improve the training.

This approach requires documentation and careful evaluation of the effects, or outcomes, of each step.

Pay close attention to clients' needs to provide high-quality work to organizations. In training, this means to assess the learning needs and preferences of potential participants, involve the participants in training evaluation, and provide other services, such as one-on-one coaching, as they apply what they learn to their everyday work.

Trainers should not use their favorite learning activities each time; they should be more flexible and adapt to different organization and learner needs. A better approach to improve training is to experiment with both the content and design of the session. If activities do not produce desired results, either change or discontinue them. Try new ways and new activities to deliver the same learning objectives.

Learn ways to evaluate training on more than one of Kirkpatrick's levels. This may include activities such as investigating how pretests and posttests can enhance learning application in a Level 2 evaluation; researching and implementing behavior assessments or interviewing learners' colleagues and supervisors to get Level 3 data; or working to understand and use performance measures before and after training, such as productivity statistics or sales figures, to conduct a Level 4 evaluation. The data gleaned from using Levels 2 through 4 of the model can provide great insight into how to improve your negotiation skills training. This is a more time-consuming method than distributing a Smile Sheet, but the pay-off can be substantial. Please see *For Further Reading* at the back of this book for additional resources on training measurement and evaluation.

When time has passed after your training, you can also solicit feedback on your competence as a trainer and facilitator. This information can help you develop as a learning professional. The root cause of less-than-optimal negotiation skills training is often the trainer, not the design. You may be interfering with the effectiveness of your sessions. Asking for feedback on what you can change is a direct way to manage your growth as a trainer, but this may not be a natural, comfortable thing for some people to do. You can become a role model for other trainers by actively engaging learners in your own quest for excellence.

What to Do Next

Here is a step-by-step method to maximize the benefits of your efforts to evaluate your negotiation skills training sessions:

- ◆ **Decide which steps to follow.** Lay out a step-by-step plan to evaluate the outcomes (impacts, pay-offs) of your negotiation skills training. Specify who will do what, when, how much, and for what purpose. Establish a timeline for these steps.

◆ **Gather feedback.** Solicit data from trainees and any other relevant people. Use the instruments included in this book to assist you in this process.

◆ **Analyze results.** Conduct both statistical and content analyses of the responses you receive as you gather data for your evaluation. Be as objective as possible during this step because you may be predisposed to use the data to validate your own opinions and observations.

◆ **Modify the design as necessary.** Your evaluation program is the beginning of your design improvement process. Use the results to strengthen what works well, and change the selection, content, or sequence of activities to reach your training objectives more effectively.

◆

Individual or Small-Group Session

What's in This Chapter?

- ◆ Advice on how to work with individuals and small groups

- ◆ How to choose the right content for training sessions

- ◆ Step-by-step preparation and training delivery instructions

- ◆ Sample agendas

The materials in this workbook are designed to meet a variety of training needs. They cover a range of topics related to negotiation skills trainees and can be offered in many different formats and timeframes. Although it is possible to enhance learning experiences and increase their depth by lengthy immersion in the learning environment, organizational realities sometimes call for training to be done in short, small doses. Organizational size and work demands may also limit the number of participants available at any particular time. This chapter discusses session designs for negotiation skills trainees individually and in small groups.

Individual Session

TRAINING OBJECTIVES

The objectives of an individual training session are to convey as much information as possible to the participant in a short time, as well as to build the one-on-one relationship between the trainer and the participant. This interaction between trainer and participant is the greatest advantage of individual training sessions. The participant's specific questions and issues can be explored in greater depth than in a session with multiple participants.

An individual training session is appropriate for these circumstances:

◆ The targeted, available audience for training is one person.

◆ One individual requires training in one particular area of content.

◆ Training facilities for multiple participants are not available.

 TIME

◆ 1 to 2 hours, 45 minutes

CHOOSING THE CONTENT

One of the advantages of training a single participant is the ability to select content specifically for an individual's needs. Although all of the content modules in this book can be used for individual training, some are more easily tailored than others. The structured experiences in this book typically require multiple participants, but some exercises may be executed by a single participant working with a trainer. The content modules most appropriate for an individual training session are:

◆ Content Module 10–2: Types of Negotiations

◆ Content Module 10–3: Negotiation Self-Assessment

◆ Content Module 10–4: Core Principles of Negotiation

◆ Content Module 10–5: Steps to Negotiating

◆ Content Module 10–7: Building Trust and Relationships

◆ Content Module 10–8: Negotiation Tactics

◆ Content Module 10–11: Negotiation Success Factors

These modules are in chapter 10.

Not all of the modules are readily adaptable to individual training sessions, but there is enough content suitable for one-on-one training to cover a wide range of negotiation skills issues. Your training needs assessment will help you to set priorities and select the content modules best suited to your audience.

The timing of certain topics is another thing to consider when you choose content. For instance, the "Types of Negotiations" module introduces us to the concept of negotiation and provides a foundation for the other modules. It should be offered first if a series of modules will be presented. The "Negotiation

Self-Assessment" module helps to focus the learning efforts of the trainee and should also be offered early in the training process. The "Core Principles of Negotiation" and "Steps to Negotiating" modules help the learner understand common practices used in negotiations, and these modules provide the learner with a specific process to negotiate effectively. They are ideally offered before the "Building Trust and Relationships," "Negotiation Tactics," and "Negotiation Success Factors" modules.

The sample agenda is designed for someone who is beginning his or her training on negotiation. It contains the "Types of Negotiations" and "Negotiation Self-Assessment" modules.

MATERIALS

For the instructor:

- This chapter for reference

- Content Module 10–2: Types of Negotiations

- Content Module 10–3: Negotiation Self-Assessment

- Structured Experience 12–1: Negotiation Partners (facilitator acts as participant's partner)

- Structured Experience 12–2: Negotiation Scenarios (facilitator helps to brainstorm scenarios)

- PowerPoint presentation: Types of Negotiations. To access slides for this program, open the file *Types of Negotiations.ppt* in the online materials. Copies of the slides for this training session are included at the end of chapter 9 (slides 9–1 through 9–12).

For the participants:

- Assessment 11–2: Negotiation Self-Assessment

- Writing instruments

- Blank paper

SAMPLE AGENDA

8:00 a.m. Introductions (5 minutes)

8:05 Content Module 10–2: Types of Negotiations (chapter 10) (1 hour, 30 minutes)

9:35 Break (10 minutes)

9:45 Content Module 10–3: Negotiation Self-Assessment (chapter 10) (1 hour)

10:45 Close

STEP-BY-STEP PLANNING

At the training session:

- Introduce yourself to the participant. Include a description of your role in the training process, as well as your training and work experience. First impressions count, and this is your chance to establish credibility with the participant.

- Ask the participant to introduce himself or herself to you, including name, role, and what the participant would like to gain from the training. Let the participant know this is an informal session and try to put him or her at ease.

- Review the agenda and learning objectives with the participant.

- Go through the selected content module(s).

- Take a break about an hour and a half after the session has begun.

- Ask whether participant has questions, and test for understanding frequently.

- Close the session with an opportunity for the participant to ask questions. If appropriate, offer your help and availability on an ongoing basis.

Small-Group Session

TRAINING OBJECTIVES

The objectives of a small-group training session are to convey as much information as possible to the participants in a short period of time, as well as to build a relationship between the trainer and the participants. The small-group setting allows in-depth discussion of a limited set of issues.

A small-group training session is appropriate for these circumstances:

- The targeted training audience consists of seven people or fewer.

◆ A few individuals require training in one particular area of content.

◆ Training facilities for large groups are not available.

TIME

◆ 1 to 2 hours, 30 minutes

CHOOSING THE CONTENT

Any of the content modules in this book can be used for small-group training. Select the module(s) based on the needs assessment of the particular group.

This sample agenda assumes that the most pressing need for this small group is to have a model they can use to improve their negotiation skills. We've selected the "Participant Introductions" and the "Steps to Negotiating" modules. The former module is an introductory exercise that helps create the learning environment by preparing the participants to act as learning partners and share commonalities of their negotiation skills. The latter module helps participants use a process with specific steps to help them negotiate more effectively, and it provides them with an opportunity to practice preparing for a negotiation conversation and explore their nonverbal communication.

MATERIALS

For the instructor:

◆ This chapter for reference

◆ Content Module 10–1: Participant Introductions

◆ Content Module 10–5: Steps to Negotiating

◆ Structured Experience 12–4: Nonverbal Negotiation

◆ Structured Experience 12–5: Preparation Practice

◆ PowerPoint presentation: Steps to Negotiating. To access slides for this program, open the file *Steps to Negotiating.ppt* in the online materials. Copies of the slides for this training session are included at the end of chapter 9 (slides 9–25 through 9–42).

For the participants:

◆ Assessment 11–7: Nonverbal Communication Self-Assessment

- ◆ Training Instrument 11–1: Negotiation Conversation Preparation Sheet

- ◆ Handout 12–1: Nonverbal Communication Chart

- ◆ Writing instruments

- ◆ Blank paper

SAMPLE AGENDA

8:00 a.m. Content Module 10–1: Participant Introductions (chapter 10) (15 minutes)

8:15 Content Module 10–5: Steps to Negotiating (chapter 10) (2 hours, 15 minutes)

10:30 Close

STEP-BY-STEP PLANNING

Just before the training session:

- ◆ Arrive early at the facility.

- ◆ Set up and test equipment (for example, laptop, projector, and flipcharts).

At the training session:

- ◆ Introduce yourself to the participants. Include a description of your role in the training process, as well as your training and work experience. First impressions count, and this is your chance to establish credibility with the participants.

- ◆ If you do not use the introductory exercise, ask the participants to introduce themselves by sharing their names, roles, and what they would like to gain from the training. Let them know they will be helping each other learn.

- ◆ Review the agenda and learning objectives with the participants.

- ◆ Go through the selected content module(s).

- ◆ Take a break about an hour after the session has begun.

- ◆ Ask whether participants have questions, and test for understanding frequently.

◆ Close the session with an opportunity for the participants to ask questions. If appropriate, offer your help and availability on an on-going basis.

What to Do Next

◆ Identify the training participant(s) and assess their most critical training needs.

◆ Determine the time available for the training session.

◆ Select the highest value content module(s) based on needs and time available.

◆ Schedule the session.

◆ Arrange a facility for the training session.

◆ Invite the participant(s).

◆ Send a confirmation to participants. Include an agenda and any advance work with the confirmation.

◆ Prepare training materials (for example, handouts, supplies, and presentations).

◆

Half-Day Session

- ◆ Advice to help choose the content for training sessions
- ◆ Step-by-step preparation and training delivery instructions
- ◆ Sample agendas

The materials in this book can be used for a variety of training needs and timeframes. This chapter covers designs suitable for half-day (three- to four-hour) training sessions. Because group training is generally more effective and enjoyable than one-on-one training sessions, try to use it whenever possible. Contributions from various participants in a group enhance the learning environment. Although group learning dynamics can be achieved with only three participants, a group of between 12 and 24 participants is best.

Objectives and Use

The objectives of a half-day training session are to build understanding of the learning content that is of greatest value to the organization and the participants, as well as to build relationships between the trainer and the participants. The group setting allows rich and diverse discussion of the various topics.

A half-day training session is appropriate for these circumstances:

- ◆ The targeted, available audience for training is three participants or more.
- ◆ The targeted audience requires training in several content areas.

- Training facilities for groups are available.

- The time available for the training session is limited to four hours.

Choosing the Content

Any of the content modules in this book can be used for half-day training sessions. Select the modules based on the needs assessment of the participant group. If the participant group has not identified a set of assessed needs (for example, if an assessment was not completed or an open registration process is being used), select the modules based on the competencies the organization seeks to develop.

Consider the order of certain topics when selecting which content will be offered first. As noted in the previous chapter, use the "Types of Negotiations" and "Negotiation Self-Assessment" modules early in the training process. The sample designs in this chapter include these modules in the first of several half-day sessions that together cover all of the book's content modules.

Note: When your training session is at least half a day, you've crossed the refreshment threshold. Hunger and thirst are enemies to the learning environment, so offer beverages and snacks at the breaks so your participants' biological needs are met.

For the first sample agenda, we've selected the "Participant Introductions," "Types of Negotiations," and "Negotiation Self-Assessment" modules.

Sample Agenda One

The "Participant Introductions" module is an introduction exercise that helps create the learning environment; it prepares the participants to act as learning partners and share common characteristics of their negotiation skills. The "Types of Negotiations" module introduces us to the concept of negotiation and sets the foundation for the rest of the negotiation skills training. The "Negotiation Self-Assessment" module helps participants recognize learning opportunities that offer the greatest leverage to improve their negotiation skills.

 TIME

- 3 hours, 15 minutes

MATERIALS

For the instructor:

- Content Module 10–1: Participant Introductions

- Content Module 10–2: Types of Negotiations

- Content Module 10–3: Negotiation Self-Assessment

- Structured Experience 12–1: Negotiation Partners

- Structured Experience 12–2: Negotiation Scenarios

- PowerPoint presentation: Types of Negotiations. To access slides for this program, open the file *Types of Negotiations.ppt* in the online materials. Copies of the slides for this training session are included at the end of chapter 9 (slides 9–1 through 9–12).

For the participants:

- Assessment 11–2: Negotiation Self-Assessment

- Writing instruments

- Blank paper

SAMPLE AGENDA

8:00 a.m.   Content Module 10–1: Participant Introductions (chapter 10) (30 minutes; varies by class size)

Objective: Prepare participants to help each other learn.

8:30   Content Module 10–2: Types of Negotiations (chapter 10) (1 hour, 30 minutes)

Objective: Understand what negotiation is and the types of negotiations individuals use for specific negotiation outcomes.

10:00   Break (10 minutes)

10:10   Content Module 10–3: Negotiation Self-Assessment (chapter 10) (1 hour)

Objective: Identify each participant's highest-impact learning opportunities.

11:10   Close (5 minutes)

               Objective: Reinforce learning points.

11:15   Participants dismissed

Sample Agenda Two

In this agenda, the "Core Principles of Negotiation" module helps participants learn about the four primary negotiation principles, as well as the ways others influence us during negotiation. Participants can also practice applying one of the principles in the learning environment. The "Investigating Interests" module looks at how important it is to find common ground during negotiation.

TIME

- 3 hours, 5 minutes

MATERIALS

For the instructor:

- Content Module 10–4: Core Principles of Negotiation

- Content Module 10–6: Investigating Interests

- Structured Experience 12–3: BATNA Basics

- Structured Experience 12–6: Brainstorming Best Practices

- PowerPoint presentation: Core Principles of Negotiation. To access slides for this program, open the file *Core Principles of Negotiation.ppt* in the online materials. Copies of the slides for this training session are included at the end of chapter 9 (slides 9–13 through 9–24).

- PowerPoint presentation: Investigating Interests. To access slides for this program, open the file *Investigating Interests.ppt* in the online materials. Copies of the slides for this training session are included at the end of chapter 9 (slides 9–43 through 9–52).

For the participants:

- Training Instrument 11–2: Brainstorming Checklist

- ♦ Writing instruments
- ♦ Blank paper

SAMPLE AGENDA

8:00 a.m. Content Module 10–4: Core Principles of Negotiation (chapter 10) (1 hour, 30 minutes)

Objective: Understand the primary principles of negotiation and ways others influence us.

9:30 Break (15 minutes)

9:45 Content Module 10–6: Investigating Interests (chapter 10) (1 hour, 15 minutes)

Objective: Understand the importance of finding common ground during negotiation.

11:00 Close (5 minutes)

Objective: Reinforce learning points.

11:05 Participants dismissed

Sample Agenda Three

This agenda covers the "Steps to Negotiating" and "Negotiation Tactics" modules. The "Steps to Negotiating" module gives participants a process with specific steps to help them negotiate more effectively, and it provides them with an opportunity to practice preparing for a negotiation conversation and explore their nonverbal communication. "Negotiation Tactics" explores some of the more commonly used tactics in negotiations and how to recognize them.

TIME

- ♦ 3 hours, 35 minutes

MATERIALS

For the instructor:

- ♦ Content Module 10–5: Steps to Negotiating
- ♦ Content Module 10–8: Negotiation Tactics

- Structured Experience 12–4: Nonverbal Negotiation

- Structured Experience 12–5: Preparation Practice

- Structured Experience 12–9: Tactics Testing

- PowerPoint presentation: Steps to Negotiating. To access slides for this program, open the file *Steps to Negotiating.ppt* in the online materials. Copies of the slides for this training session are included at the end of chapter 9 (slides 9–25 through 9–42).

- PowerPoint presentation: Negotiation Tactics. To access slides for this program, open the file *Negotiation Tactics.ppt* in the online materials. Copies of the slides for this training session are included at the end of chapter 9 (slides 9–63 through 9–70).

For the participants:

- Assessment 11–7: Nonverbal Communication Self-Assessment

- Training Instrument 11–1: Negotiation Conversation Preparation Sheet

- Handout 12–1: Nonverbal Communication Chart

- Handout 12–2: Common Negotiation Tactics

- Candy or other small prizes (optional)

- Writing instruments

- Blank paper

SAMPLE AGENDA

8:00 a.m.   Content Module 10–5: Steps to Negotiating (chapter 10) (2 hours, 15 minutes)

Objective: Use a process to negotiate more effectively and practice preparing for a negotiation conversation.

10:15   Break (15 minutes)

10:30   Content Module 10–8: Negotiation Tactics (chapter 10) (1 hour)

Objective: Identify and demonstrate understanding of common negotiation tactics and how to recognize their use.

11:30   Close (5 minutes)

Objective: Reinforce learning points.

11:35   Participants dismissed

Sample Agenda Four

This agenda contains two modules: "Building Trust and Relationships" and "Barriers to Negotiation."

TIME

◆ 3 hours, 35 minutes

MATERIALS

For the instructor:

◆ Content Module 10–7: Building Trust and Relationships

◆ Content Module 10–9: Barriers to Negotiation

◆ Structured Experience 12–7: Out of the Question

◆ Structured Experience 12–8: A Different Point of View

◆ Structured Experience 12–10: Beyond the Barriers

◆ PowerPoint presentation: Building Trust and Relationships. To access slides for this program, open the file *Building Trust and Relationships.ppt* in the online materials. Copies of the slides for this training session are included at the end of chapter 9 (slides 9–53 through 9–62).

◆ PowerPoint presentation: Barriers to Negotiation. To access slides for this program, open the file *Barriers to Negotiation.ppt* in the online materials. Copies of the slides for this training session are included at the end of chapter 9 (slides 9–71 through 9–80).

For the participants:

◆ Handout 12–3: Barrier Role-Play Scenarios

◆ Writing instruments

◆ Blank paper

SAMPLE AGENDA

8:00 a.m.	Content Module 10–7: Building Trust and Relationships (chapter 10) (2 hours)
	Objective: Explore asking questions and analyzing others' points of view to build good relationships during negotiation.
10:00	Break (15 minutes)
10:15	Content Module 10–9: Barriers to Negotiation (chapter 10) (1 hour, 15 minutes)
	Objective: Demonstrate understanding of various obstacles to negotiation situations and how to deal with them.
11:30	Close (5 minutes)
	Objective: Reinforce learning points.
11:35	Participants dismissed

Sample Agenda Five

This agenda contains the remaining modules, "Ethics in Negotiation" and "Negotiation Success Factors."

TIME

◆ 3 hours, 5 minutes

MATERIALS

For the instructor:

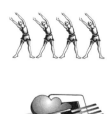

◆ Content Module 10–10: Ethics in Negotiation

◆ Content Module 10–11: Negotiation Success Factors

◆ Structured Experience 12–11: Examining Ethics

◆ Structured Experience 12–12: What a Success!

◆ PowerPoint presentation: Ethics in Negotiation. To access slides for this program, open the file *Ethics in Negotiation.ppt* in the online materials. Copies of the slides for this training session are included at the end of chapter 9 (slides 9–81 through 9–90).

◆ PowerPoint presentation: Negotiation Success Factors. To access slides for this program, open the file *Negotiation Success Factors.ppt* in the online materials. Copies of the slides for this training session are included at the end of chapter 9 (slides 9–91 through 9–102).

For the participants:

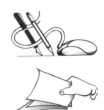

◆ Training Instrument 11–3: Negotiation Success Plan

◆ Handout 12–4: Ethics Case Study

◆ Writing instruments

SAMPLE AGENDA

8:00 a.m.   Content Module 10–10: Ethics in Negotiation (chapter 10) (1 hour, 30 minutes)

Objective: Examine ethical issues in negotiations and approaches to ethical dilemmas.

9:30   Break (15 minutes)

9:45   Content Module 10–11: Negotiation Success Factors (chapter 10) (1 hour, 15 minutes)

Objective: Apply effective measures and criteria to a negotiation success plan.

11:00   Close (5 minutes)

Objective: Reinforce learning points.

11:05   Participants dismissed

Step-by-Step Planning

Just before the training session:

◆ Arrive early at the facility.

◆ Set up and test equipment (for example, laptop, projector, and flipcharts).

◆ Confirm refreshments.

At the training session:

- Introduce yourself to the participants. Include a description of your role in the training process, as well as your training and work experience. First impressions count, and this is your chance to establish credibility with the participants.

- If you do not use the participant introduction exercise, ask the participants to introduce themselves by sharing their names, roles, and what they would like to gain from the training. Let them know they will be helping each other learn.

- Review the agenda and learning objectives with the participants.

- Go through the selected content modules.

- Ask whether participants have questions, and test for understanding frequently.

- Close the session with an opportunity for the participants to ask questions. If appropriate, offer your help and availability on an ongoing basis.

At the second through fifth sessions:

- Review the agenda and learning objectives with the participants.

- Go through the selected content modules.

- Ask whether participants have questions, and test for understanding frequently.

- Close the session with an opportunity for the participants to ask questions. If appropriate, offer your help and availability on an ongoing basis.

What to Do Next

- Identify the training participants. Assess their most critical training needs, or identify the competencies the organization seeks to develop.

- Determine the agenda using the highest value content modules based on your needs assessment or the required competencies.

- Schedule the session.

- Arrange a facility for the training session.

◆ Invite participants.

◆ Send a confirmation to participants. Include an agenda and any pre-work with the confirmation.

◆ Prepare training materials (for example, handouts, presentations, and exercise materials).

◆ Order food and beverages.

◆

Full-Day Session

What's in This Chapter?

- ◆ Advice on how to choose the content for training sessions
- ◆ Step-by-step preparation and training delivery instructions
- ◆ Sample agendas

The materials in this book have been designed to meet a variety of training needs and timeframes. This chapter covers designs suitable for full-day (six- to eight-hour) training sessions.

Full-day training experiences, and those that are even longer, might raise concerns that participants will be overloaded with information. Nevertheless, the benefits of extended learning experiences can outweigh the potential drawbacks. A shorter program might be seen as part of a typical workday, but a longer program can become a memorable life experience for the participant, especially if it is held at an offsite venue. Participants often need a different physical environment and a complete break from daily routine to focus on learning. It's easier to create the learning environment discussed in chapter 4 in extended programs that can thoroughly explore the various negotiation skills competencies. Full-day sessions are appropriate for group training, and the backgrounds and experiences of a variety of participants enhance the learning environment. For full-day sessions, a group of between 12 and 24 participants is best.

Although this chapter includes illustrative designs, the trainer should adapt them to fit the training purposes. Each design can be modified to take into account the resources available, the learning readiness of potential participants, and, above all, the assessed development needs of the learners and the organization.

Objectives and Use

The objectives of a full-day training session are to free participants from their daily routine so they can understand the learning content that is of greatest value, as well as to build relationships between the trainer and the participants. The group setting allows for rich and diverse discussion of the various topics.

A full-day training session is appropriate for these circumstances:

- ◆ The targeted, available audience for training is 12 participants or more.

- ◆ The targeted audience requires training in several content areas.

- ◆ Training facilities for groups are available.

- ◆ A full day is available for the training session.

- ◆ Funding for meals (and optionally) for an offsite location is available.

Choosing the Content

Any of the content modules in this book can be used as part of a full-day training session. Select the modules based on the needs assessment of the participant group. If the needs have not been identified for the group (either an assessment was not completed, or an open registration process is being used), select the modules based on the competencies the organization seeks to develop.

As noted for half-day sessions, the entire curriculum contained in this book can also be offered in a series of full-day sessions.

 When your training session is at least a full day, you've crossed over the meal threshold. Hunger and thirst are enemies to the learning environment, so offer beverages and snacks at the breaks so your participants' biological needs are met. Provide lunch, and keep the participants together during the lunch break to encourage them to continue their discussion of learning points. This also helps to strengthen the relationships between participants, which helps support the learning environment. A scheduled lunch break is beneficial in other ways: Participants are less likely to go back to the office and get distracted from their learning focus, and they are also less likely to come back late from the lunch break, which helps to keep your session on schedule.

Three sample agendas are included. Each is designed as a stand-alone training session and reflects a different major training issue about negotiation skills.

Sample Agenda One

This agenda reflects a requirement for training about basic negotiation skills and how participants can learn by following a specific process. This may have been identified as an organizational competency or as a common need for the participants. The timing of the "Types of Negotiations" and "Steps to Negotiating" modules assumes that both structured experiences for the modules are conducted and that the workshop facilitator determines the exact allocation of time.

TIME

  ♦ 7 hours, 30 minutes

MATERIALS

For the instructor:

  ♦ Content Module 10–1: Participant Introductions

  ♦ Content Module 10–2: Types of Negotiations

  ♦ Content Module 10–4: Core Principles of Negotiation

  ♦ Content Module 10–5: Steps to Negotiating

  ♦ Structured Experience 12–1: Negotiation Partners

  ♦ Structured Experience 12–2: Negotiation Scenarios

  ♦ Structured Experience 12–3: BATNA Basics

  ♦ Structured Experience 12–4: Nonverbal Negotiation

  ♦ Structured Experience 12–5: Preparation Practice

  ♦ PowerPoint presentation: Types of Negotiations. To access slides for this program, open the file *Types of Negotiations.ppt* in the online materials. Copies of the slides for this training session are included at the end of chapter 9 (slides 9–1 through 9–12).

  ♦ PowerPoint presentation: Core Principles of Negotiation. To access slides for this program, open the file *Core Principles of Negotiation.ppt*

in the online materials. Copies of the slides for this training session are included at the end of chapter 9 (slides 9–13 through 9–24).

◆ PowerPoint presentation: Steps to Negotiating. To access slides for this program, open the file *Steps to Negotiating.ppt* in the online materials. Copies of the slides for this training session are included at the end of chapter 9 (slides 9–25 through 9–42).

For the participants:

◆ Assessment 11–7: Nonverbal Communication Self-Assessment

◆ Training Instrument 11–1: Negotiation Conversation Preparation Sheet

◆ Handout 12–1: Nonverbal Communication Chart

◆ Writing instruments

◆ Blank paper

SAMPLE AGENDA

8:00 a.m.   Content Module 10–1: Participant Introductions (chapter 10) (45 minutes; varies by class size)

Objective: Prepare participants to help each other learn.

8:45   Content Module 10–2: Types of Negotiations (chapter 10) (1 hour, 30 minutes)

Objective: Understand what negotiation is and the types of negotiations individuals use for specific negotiation outcomes.

10:15   Break (15 minutes)

10:30   Content Module 10–4: Core Principles of Negotiation (chapter 10) (1 hour, 30 minutes)

Objective: Understand the primary principles of negotiation and ways that others influence us.

12:00 p.m.   Lunch (1 hour)

1:00   Begin Content Module 10–5: Steps to Negotiating (chapter 10) (1 hour)

Objective: Use a process to negotiate more effectively and practice preparing for a negotiation conversation.

2:00   Break (10 minutes)

2:10   Continue Content Module 10–5: Steps to Negotiating (1 hour, 15 minutes)

3:25   Close (5 minutes)

Objective: Reinforce learning points.

3:30   Participants dismissed

Sample Agenda Two

This agenda is based on an identified need to improve the ability of learners to negotiate more effectively and to be aware of their particular behaviors during negotiation.

TIME

◆ 7 hours, 20 minutes

MATERIALS

For the instructor:

◆ Content Module 10–1: Participant Introductions

◆ Content Module 10–2: Types of Negotiations

◆ Content Module 10–3: Negotiation Self-Assessment

◆ Content Module 10–8: Negotiation Tactics

◆ Content Module 10–10: Ethics in Negotiation

◆ Structured Experience 12–1: Negotiation Partners

◆ Structured Experience 12–2: Negotiation Scenarios

◆ Structured Experience 12–9: Tactics Testing

◆ Structured Experience 12–11: Examining Ethics

- PowerPoint presentation: Types of Negotiations. To access slides for this program, open the file *Types of Negotiations.ppt* in the online materials. Copies of the slides for this training session are included at the end of chapter 9 (slides 9–1 through 9–12).

- PowerPoint presentation: Negotiation Tactics. To access slides for this program, open the file *Negotiation Tactics.ppt* in the online materials. Copies of the slides for this training session are included at the end of chapter 9 (slides 9–63 through 9–70).

- PowerPoint presentation: Ethics in Negotiation. To access slides for this program, open the file *Ethics in Negotiation.ppt* in the online materials. Copies of the slides for this training session are included at the end of chapter 9 (slides 9–81 through 9–90).

For the participants:

- Assessment 11–2: Negotiation Self-Assessment

- Handout 12–2: Common Negotiation Tactics

- Handout 12–4: Ethics Case Study

- Candy or other small prizes (optional)

- Writing instruments

- Blank paper

SAMPLE AGENDA

8:00 a.m.   Content Module 10–1: Participant Introductions (chapter 10) (45 minutes; varies by class size)

Objective: Prepare participants to help each other learn.

8:45   Content Module 10–2: Types of Negotiations (chapter 10) (1 hour, 30 minutes)

Objective: Understand what negotiation is and the types of negotiations individuals use for specific negotiation outcomes.

10:15   Break (15 minutes)

10:30   Content Module 10–3: Negotiation Self-Assessment (chapter 10) (1 hour)

Objective: Identify each participant's highest impact learning.

11:30   Lunch (1 hour)

12:30 p.m.   Content Module 10–8: Negotiation Tactics (chapter 10) (1 hour)

Objective: Identify and demonstrate understanding of common negotiation tactics and how to recognize their use.

1:30   Break (15 minutes)

1:45   Content Module 10–10: Ethics in Negotiation (chapter 10) (1 hour, 30 minutes)

Objective: Examine ethical issues in negotiations and approaches to ethical dilemmas.

3:15   Close (5 minutes)

Objective: Reinforce learning points.

3:20   Participants dismissed

Sample Agenda Three

This agenda is designed to strengthen the relationship-building and negotiation skills of the participants.

TIME

◆ 8 hours, 5 minutes

MATERIALS

For the instructor:

◆ Content Module 10–1: Participant Introductions

◆ Content Module 10–6: Investigating Interests

◆ Content Module 10–7: Building Trust and Relationships

◆ Content Module 10–9: Barriers to Negotiation

◆ Content Module 10–11: Negotiation Success Factors

◆ Structured Experience 12–6: Brainstorming Best Practices

◆ Structured Experience 12–7: Out of the Question

- Structured Experience 12–8: A Different Point of View

- Structured Experience 12–10: Beyond the Barriers

- Structured Experience 12–12: What a Success!

- PowerPoint presentation: Investigating Interests. To access slides for this program, open the file *Investigating Interests.ppt* in the online materials. Copies of the slides for this training session are included at the end of chapter 9 (slides 9–43 through 9–52).

- PowerPoint presentation: Building Trust and Relationships. To access slides for this program, open the file *Building Trust and Relationships.ppt* in the online materials. Copies of the slides for this training session are included at the end of chapter 9 (slides 9–53 through 9–62).

- PowerPoint presentation: Barriers to Negotiation. To access slides for this program, open the file *Barriers to Negotiation.ppt* in the online materials. Copies of the slides for this training session are included at the end of chapter 9 (slides 9–71 through 9–80).

- PowerPoint presentation: Negotiation Success Factors. To access slides for this program, open the file *Negotiation Success Factors.ppt* in the online materials. Copies of the slides for this training session are included at the end of chapter 9 (slides 9–91 through 9–102).

For the participants:

- Training Instrument 11–2: Brainstorming Checklist

- Training Instrument 11–3: Negotiation Success Plan

- Handout 12–3: Barrier Role-Play Scenarios

- Writing instruments

- Blank paper

SAMPLE AGENDA

8:00 a.m.	Content Module 10–1: Participant Introductions (chapter 10) (45 minutes; varies by class size)
	Objective: Prepare participants to help each other learn.
8:45	Content Module 10–6: Investigating Interests (chapter 10) (1 hour, 15 minutes)

Objective: Understand the importance of finding common ground during negotiation.

10:00   Break (15 minutes)

10:15   Begin Content Module 10–7: Building Trust and Relationships (chapter 10) (1 hour)

Objective: Explore asking questions and analyzing others' points of view to build good relationships during negotiation.

11:15   Lunch (1 hour)

12:15 p.m.   Continue Content Module 10–7: Building Trust and Relationships (chapter 10) (1 hour)

1:15   Content Module 10–9: Barriers to Negotiation (chapter 10) (1 hour, 15 minutes)

Objective: Demonstrate understanding of various obstacles to negotiation situations and how to deal with them.

2:30   Break (15 minutes)

2:45   Content Module 10–11: Negotiation Success Factors (chapter 10) (1 hour, 15 minutes)

Objective: Apply effective measures and criteria to a negotiation success plan.

4:00   Close (5 Minutes)

Objective: Reinforce learning points.

4:05   Participants dismissed

Step-by-Step Planning

Just before the training session:

- ◆ Arrive early at the facility.

- ◆ Set up and test equipment (for example, laptop, projector, and flipcharts).

- ◆ Confirm refreshments.

At the training session:

- Introduce yourself to the participants. Include a description of your role in the training process, as well as your training and work experience. First impressions count, and this is your chance to establish credibility with the participants.

- If you do not use the participant introduction exercise, ask the participants to introduce themselves by sharing their names, roles, and what they would like to gain from the training. Let them know they will be helping each other learn.

- Review the agenda and learning objectives with the participants.

- Go through the selected content modules.

- Ask participants whether they have questions, and test for understanding frequently.

- Close the session with an opportunity for the participants to ask questions. If appropriate, offer your help and availability on an on-going basis.

What to Do Next

- Identify the training participants. Assess their most critical training needs or identify the competencies the organization seeks to develop.

- Determine the agenda using the highest value content modules based on your needs assessment or the required competencies.

- Schedule the session.

- Arrange a facility for the training session.

- Invite participants. Check to see if anyone has special dietary needs.

- Send a confirmation to participants. Include an agenda and any pre-work with the confirmation.

- Prepare training materials (for example, handouts, presentations, and exercise materials).

- Order food and beverages.

◆

Chapter 9

Multiday Session

- ◆ Advice on how to choose the content for training sessions
- ◆ Step-by-step preparation and training delivery instructions
- ◆ Sample agendas

The materials in this book have been designed to meet a variety of training needs and timeframes. This chapter covers designs suitable for day-and-a-half and two-day training sessions.

As noted in chapter 8, longer learning experiences might raise concerns that participants will be overloaded with information. To avoid this, design programs that allow participants to learn efficiently and at their own pace. The purpose of this chapter is to present a significant amount of content in a multiday session by mixing short, to-the-point theory and models with experiential exercises and assessments. This prevents the participants from feeling overwhelmed and, instead, produces an enjoyable, fruitful learning experience.

In addition, extended learning experiences can be beneficial. Although a shorter program might be considered part of a typical workday, a longer program can become a memorable life experience for the participant, especially if it is held at an off-site venue and includes an overnight stay. A multiday design provides ample opportunity to create the learning environment (as discussed in chapter 4) and establish participants as learning partners. Discussion during breaks, meals, and evening activities often provides valuable feedback and learning. Participants often need a different physical environment and a complete break from daily routine to focus on learning.

Multiday sessions are appropriate for group training, and the backgrounds and experiences of a variety of participants enhance the learning environment. For multiday sessions, groups of between 12 and 24 participants are best. Smaller groups can limit the richness of group interactions, and larger groups can become unwieldy for the facilitator and can depersonalize the learning experience.

Please note that although illustrative designs are included, the trainer should adapt them to fit his or her specific purposes. Each design can be modified to take into account the available resources, the learning readiness of potential participants, and, above all, the assessed development needs of the target audience.

Objectives and Use

The objectives of a multiday training session are to free participants from their daily routines so they can understand the learning content that is of greatest value, as well as build relationships between the trainer and the participants. The group setting and time available for interaction allow rich and diverse discussion of the various topics.

Note: Residential programs held at appealing off-site facilities can also be used to create a special learning experience.

A multiday training session is appropriate for these circumstances:

- ◆ The targeted, available audience for training is 12 participants or more.

- ◆ The targeted audience requires comprehensive training in all areas of relevant content.

- ◆ Training facilities for groups are available.

- ◆ Participants are available for multiple days.

- ◆ Funding is available for meals and possibly an off-site location.

Choosing the Content

Any of the content modules in this book can be used for multiday training sessions. Although a multiday session allows time to cover all of the content modules, you may still need to perform a needs assessment of the participant group or review the competencies the organization seeks to develop. Include only those modules indicated by your needs assessment.

With a session that covers multiple days, you have to consider providing meals and possibly overnight accommodations. Hunger and thirst are enemies to the learning environment, so offer beverages and snacks at the breaks, as well as meals at appropriate times, to ensure that your participants' biological needs are met. Keep participants together during meals to encourage relationships between participants, which helps support the learning environment. Much discussion and feedback occurs during dinner after a long day of training. As noted in chapter 8, scheduled meals are beneficial in other ways: Participants are less likely to go back to the office and get distracted from their learning focus, and they are also less likely to come back late from the lunch break, which helps to keep your session on schedule.

All of the content modules in this book are included in one of the following sample agendas. The timing of the modules assumes that all of the structured experiences will be included.

The placement of the "Participant Introductions," "Types of Negotiations," and "Negotiation Self-Assessment" modules is important. They should be offered at the beginning of the session because they create the context for the remaining content modules, which helps focus the participants' learning.

Sample Agenda, Day One

TIME

   ◆   8.5 hours of instructional time

MATERIALS

For the instructor:

   ◆   Content Module 10–1: Participant Introductions

   ◆   Content Module 10–2: Types of Negotiations

   ◆   Content Module 10–3: Negotiation Self-Assessment

   ◆   Content Module 10–4: Core Principles of Negotiation

   ◆   Content Module 10–5: Steps to Negotiation

- Structured Experience 12–1: Negotiation Partners

- Structured Experience 12–2: Negotiation Scenarios

- Structured Experience 12–3: BATNA Basics

- Structured Experience 12–4: Nonverbal Negotiation

- Structured Experience 12–5: Preparation Practice

- PowerPoint presentation: Types of Negotiations. To access slides for this program, open the file *Types of Negotiations.ppt* in the online materials. Copies of the slides for this training session are included at the end of chapter 9 (slides 9–1 through 9–12).

- PowerPoint presentation: Core Principles of Negotiation. To access slides for this program, open the file *Core Principles of Negotiation.ppt* in the online materials. Copies of the slides for this training session are included at the end of chapter 9 (slides 9–13 through 9–24).

- PowerPoint presentation: Steps to Negotiating. To access slides for this program, open the file *Steps to Negotiating.ppt* in the online materials. Copies of the slides for this training session are included at the end of chapter 9 (slides 9–25 through 9–42).

For the participants:

- Assessment 11–2: Negotiation Self-Assessment

- Assessment 11–7: Nonverbal Communication Self-Assessment

- Training Instrument 11–1: Negotiation Conversation Preparation Sheet

- Handout 12–1: Nonverbal Communication Chart

- Writing instruments

- Blank paper

SAMPLE AGENDA

8:00 a.m. Content Module 10–1: Participant Introductions (chapter 10) (45 minutes; varies by class size)

Objective: Prepare participants to help each other learn.

8:45 Content Module 10–2: Types of Negotiations (chapter 10) (1 hour, 30 minutes)

Objective: Understand what negotiation is and the types of negotiations that individuals use for specific negotiation outcomes.

10:15   Break (15 minutes)

10:30   Content Module 10–3: Negotiation Self-Assessment (chapter 10) (1 hour)

Objective: Identify each participant's highest impact learning.

11:30   Lunch (1 hour)

12:30 p.m.   Content Module 10–4: Core Principles of Negotiation (chapter 10) (1 hour, 30 minutes)

Objective: Understand the primary principles of negotiation and ways that others influence us.

2:00   Break (15 minutes)

2:15   Content Module 10–5: Steps to Negotiation (chapter 10) (2 hours, 15 minutes)

4:30   Close (5 minutes)

Objective: Reinforce learning points.

4:35   Break (1 hour, 25 minutes)

6:00   Optional dinner (if at an off-site location)

7:00   Optional after-dinner activities (if at a residential off-site location)

Sample Agenda, Day Two (Full-Day Option)

TIME

- ◆ 8 hours, 20 minutes

MATERIALS

For the instructor:

- ◆ Content Module 10–6: Investigating Interests

- ◆ Content Module 10–7: Building Trust and Relationships

- Content Module 10–8: Negotiation Tactics

- Content Module 10–9: Barriers to Negotiation

- Content Module 10–11: Negotiation Success Factors

- Structured Experience 12–6: Brainstorming Best Practices

- Structured Experience 12–7: Out of the Question

- Structured Experience 12–8: A Different Point of View

- Structured Experience 12–9: Tactics Testing

- Structured Experience 12–10: Beyond the Barriers

- Structured Experience 12–12: What a Success!

- PowerPoint presentation: Investigating Interests. To access slides for this program, open the file *Investigating Interests.ppt* in the online materials. Copies of the slides for this training session are included at the end of chapter 9 (slides 9–43 through 9–52).

- PowerPoint presentation: Building Trust and Relationships. To access slides for this program, open the file *Building Trust and Relationships.ppt* in the online materials. Copies of the slides for this training session are included at the end of chapter 9 (slides 9–53 through 9–62).

- PowerPoint presentation: Negotiation Tactics. To access slides for this program, open the file *Negotiation Tactics.ppt* in the online materials. Copies of the slides for this training session are included at the end of chapter 9 (slides 9–63 through 9–70).

- PowerPoint presentation: Barriers to Negotiation. To access slides for this program, open the file *Barriers to Negotiation.ppt* in the online materials. Copies of the slides for this training session are included at the end of chapter 9 (slides 9–71 through 9–80).

- PowerPoint presentation: Negotiation Success Factors. To access slides for this program, open the file *Negotiation Success Factors.ppt* in the online materials. Copies of the slides for this training session are included at the end of chapter 9 (slides 9–91 through 9–102).

For the participants:

- Training Instrument 11–2: Brainstorming Checklist

- Training Instrument 11–3: Negotiation Success Plan

- ◆ Handout 12–2: Common Negotiation Tactics

- ◆ Handout 12-3: Barrier Role-Play Scenarios

- ◆ Candy or other small prizes (optional)

- ◆ Writing instruments

- ◆ Blank paper

SAMPLE AGENDA

8:00 a.m.   Content Module 10-6: Investigating Interests (chapter 10) (1 hour, 15 minutes)

Objective: Understand the importance of finding common ground during negotiation.

9:15   Break (15 minutes)

9:30   Content Module 10–7: Building Trust and Relationships (chapter 10) (2 hours)

Objective: Ask questions and analyze others' points of view to build good relationships during negotiation.

11:30   Lunch (1 hour)

12:30 p.m.   Content Module 10–8: Negotiation Tactics (chapter 10) (1 hour)

Objective: Identify and demonstrate understanding of common negotiation tactics and how to recognize their use.

1:30   Content Module 10–9: Barriers to Negotiation (chapter 10) (1 hour, 15 minutes)

Objective: Demonstrate understanding of various obstacles to negotiation situations and how to deal with them.

2:45   Break (15 minutes)

3:00   Content Module 10–11: Negotiation Success Factors (chapter 10) (1 hour, 15 minutes)

Objective: Apply effective measures and criteria to a negotiation success plan.

4:15   Close (5 minutes)

                Objective: Reinforce learning points.

4:20   Participants dismissed

Sample Agenda, Day Two (Half-Day Option)

TIME

- 3 hours, 5 minutes

MATERIALS

For the instructor:

- Content Module 10–10: Ethics in Negotiation

- Content Module 10–11: Negotiation Success Factors

- Structured Experience 12–11: Examining Ethics

- Structured Experience 12–12: What a Success!

- PowerPoint presentation: Ethics in Negotiation. To access slides for this program, open the file *Ethics in Negotiation.ppt* in the online materials. Copies of the slides for this training session are included at the end of chapter 9 (slides 9–81 through 9–90).

- PowerPoint presentation: Negotiation Success Factors. To access slides for this program, open the file *Negotiation Success Factors.ppt* in the online materials. Copies of the slides for this training session are included at the end of chapter 9 (slides 9–91 through 9–102).

For the participants:

- Training Instrument 11–3: Negotiation Success Plan

- Handout 12–4: Ethics Case Study

- Writing instruments

- Blank paper

SAMPLE AGENDA

8:00 a.m. Content Module 10-10: Ethics in Negotiation (chapter 10) (1 hour, 30 minutes)

Objective: Examine ethical issues in negotiations and approaches to ethical dilemmas.

9:30 Break (15 minutes)

9:45 Content Module 10–11: Negotiation Success Factors (chapter 10) (1 hour, 15 minutes)

Objective: Apply effective measures and criteria to a negotiation success plan.

11:00 Close (5 minutes)

Objective: Reinforce learning points.

11:05 Participants dismissed

Step-by-Step Planning

Just before the training session:

- If this is a residential program, confirm rooming list with hotel.

- Arrive early at the facility.

- Set up and test equipment (for example, laptop, projector, and flipcharts).

- Confirm refreshments.

At the training session:

- Introduce yourself to the participants. Include a description of your role in the training process and your training and work experience. First impressions count, and this is your chance to establish credibility with the participants.

- If you do not use the participant introduction exercise, ask the participants to introduce themselves by sharing their names, roles, and what they would like to gain from the training. Let them know they will be helping each other learn.

- Review each day's agenda and learning objectives with the participants.

- Go through the selected content modules.

- Ask participants if they have questions, and test for understanding frequently.

- Close each day with an opportunity for the participants to ask questions.

What to Do Next

- Identify the training participants. Assess their most critical training needs or identify the competencies the organization seeks to develop.

- Design the agenda using the highest value content modules based on your needs assessment or the required competencies.

- Schedule the session.

- Arrange a facility for the training session. Book a block of rooms if this is a residential program.

- Invite participants. Check for any special dietary needs. If this is a residential program, check for rooming requirements (smoking/non-smoking, single/double bed, and so forth).

- Send a confirmation to participants. Include an agenda and any pre-work with the confirmation.

- Prepare training materials (for example, handouts, presentations, and exercise materials).

- Order food and beverages.

Slide 9–1

Types of Negotiations

Lisa J. Downs

American Society for Training & Development

Slide 9–2

To Negotiate Is To...

- Use interpersonal communication effectively to achieve desired outcomes.
- Explore common interests, needs, and differences.
- Reach mutual agreement.

Slide 9–3

Negotiation Types

- Adversarial (or Positional): A gain by one side is typically at the expense of the other; contest of wills.
- Interest-Based (or Principled): Value for both sides is created through weaving common interests; decision is based on merit.

Slide 9–4

Negotiation Types

In Adversarial Negotiation...

- Focus is on who will get the most out of the deal.
- A fixed value is at stake.
- Competition is key.

What are your experiences or examples with this negotiation type?

Slide 9–5

Negotiation Types

In Interest-Based Negotiation...

- Focus is on achieving maximum gain for both sides.
- Value is both created and claimed for yourself.
- Cooperation is key.

What are your experiences or examples with this negotiation type?

Slide 9–6

Common Negotiation Outcomes

- Lose-Lose
- Win-Lose
- Win-Win
- No Result

Source: Stark, Peter B., and Jane Flaherty. *The Only Negotiating Guide You'll Ever Need: 101 Ways to Win Every Time in Any Situation.* New York: Broadway Books, 2003.

Slide 9–7

Common Negotiation Outcomes

Lose-Lose:

Neither side achieves its needs or wants; distrust typically is involved.

Example: involved in a labor strike

Source: Stark, Peter B., and Jane Flaherty. *The Only Negotiating Guide You'll Ever Need: 101 Ways to Win Every Time in Any Situation.* New York: Broadway Books, 2003.

Slide 9–8

Common Negotiation Outcomes

Win-Lose (or Lose-Win):

Only one side gets its needs or wants met; concessions are made.

Example: stuck with a faulty product

Source: Stark, Peter B., and Jane Flaherty. *The Only Negotiating Guide You'll Ever Need: 101 Ways to Win Every Time in Any Situation.* New York: Broadway Books, 2003.

Slide 9–9

Common Negotiation Outcomes

Win-Win:

The needs and wants of both sides are met; leads to positive feelings.

Example: secure favorable terms for a loan

Source: Stark, Peter B., and Jane Flaherty. *The Only Negotiating Guide You'll Ever Need: 101 Ways to Win Every Time in Any Situation.* New York: Broadway Books, 2003.

Slide 9–10

Common Negotiation Outcomes

No Result:

Neither side wins or loses; there is a willingness to negotiate again in the future.

Example: walk away from a car deal

Source: Stark, Peter B., and Jane Flaherty. *The Only Negotiating Guide You'll Ever Need: 101 Ways to Win Every Time in Any Situation.* New York: Broadway Books, 2003.

Slide 9–11

Common Negotiation Outcomes

Questions to Consider:

- Is Win-Win *really* possible?
- Can both sides get *everything* they want?
- Don't *some* trade-offs have to be made?

Slide 9–12

Common Negotiation Outcomes

Success Factors for Win-Win:

- Explore a counterpart's needs rather than assume them.
- Bring multiple issues to the negotiation rather than just one.
- Consider that your needs may be different from theirs.

Slide 9–13

Core Principles of Negotiation

Lisa J. Downs

American Society for Training & Development

Slide 9–14

Four Core Principles

- BATNA
- ZOPA
- Wants Versus Needs
- Empathy

Slide 9–15

BATNA

- Defined by Roger Fisher and William Ury as the *Best Alternative To a Negotiated Agreement*
- Involves knowing what you will or won't do if an agreement isn't reached
- Helps you gauge when to walk away and when a deal makes sense

Source: Watkins, Michael. *Negotiation.* Boston: Harvard Business School Press, 2003.

Slide 9–16

Knowing Your BATNA

- Decide your BATNA *before* you enter into a negotiation; make it strong.
- Work to identify your counterpart's BATNA.
- Improve your BATNA by seeking alternatives that don't require the other side's cooperation; have less to lose.

Source: Watkins, Michael. *Negotiation.* Boston, Massachusetts: Harvard Business School Press, 2003.

Slide 9–17

ZOPA

- Defined as the *Zone Of Possible Agreement*
- The set of agreements that can satisfy both sides in a negotiation
- Assumes overlap of needs and wants to create a range of acceptable terms

Source: Watkins, Michael. *Negotiation.* Boston, Massachusetts: Harvard Business School Press, 2003.

Slide 9–18

Creating Your ZOPA

- Determine your ZOPA (i.e., a high and low range of acceptable terms) *before* you enter into a negotiation.
- Work to identify your counterpart's ZOPA.
- Consider all elements of value to both sides; have something in reserve to "sweeten" a deal, if necessary.

Source: Watkins, Michael. *Negotiation.* Boston: Harvard Business School Press, 2003.

Slide 9–19

Wants Versus Needs

- Want = A desired outcome of the negotiation; one side's belief of the best way to solve a problem
- Need = A "must" for the negotiation to be a success; underlying interest
- The key is to explore options without compromising needs.

Source: Gosselin, Tom. *Practical Negotiating: Tools, Tactics and Techniques*. Hoboken, New Jersey: John Wiley and Sons, Inc., 2007.

Slide 9–20

Identifying Wants Versus Needs

- Engage in a process of discovery by asking your counterpart questions.
- Be honest about your wants and needs and encourage the same honesty from the other side.
- Pay attention to both *explicit* needs (verbalized) and *implicit* needs (emotions).

Source: Gosselin, Tom. *Practical Negotiating: Tools, Tactics and Techniques*. Hoboken, New Jersey: John Wiley and Sons, Inc., 2007.

Slide 9–21

Empathy

- Involves understanding your counterpart's view and goals.
- Leads to a focus on common interests and joint problem-solving.
- Leads to enhanced interdependence and trust.

Slide 9–22

Using Empathy in Negotiation

- Recognize emotions—both yours and theirs; seek to understand them.
- Listen carefully and pay close attention.
- Identify interests by asking questions.
- Focus on the problem and look forward for a solution.

Slide 9–23

Principles of Influence

- Reciprocity: Give and take; can lead you to feel obligated and agree to unfair deals because you "owe" the other side.
- Social Proof: Decisions based on what others think is best; may not necessarily be the best course of action.

Source: Cialdini, Dr. Robert B. *Influence: The Psychology of Persuasion* (Collins Business Essentials Edition). New York: Harper Collins, 2007.

Slide 9–24

Principles of Influence

- Liking: We tend to say "yes" to people we like; can lead to a sense of duty based on superficial factors (e.g., looks, personality).
- Scarcity: Opportunities seem more valuable to us when availability is limited; potential loss is key to decision making.

Source: Cialdini, Dr. Robert B. *Influence: The Psychology of Persuasion* (Collins Business Essentials Edition). New York: Harper Collins, 2007.

Slide 9–25

Steps to Negotiation

Lisa J. Downs

American Society for Training & Development

Slide 9–26

Negotiation Steps

1. Analysis
2. Preparation
3. Communication
4. Proposal
5. Commitment

Slide 9–27

Step 1: Analysis

- Diagnose the negotiation situation (i.e., determine the issue at hand).
- Clarify the facts about the issue.
- Note barriers to resolving the issue.
- Examine the wants and needs of the other side in relation to yours.

Source: Fisher, Roger, William Ury, and Bruce Patton, editor. *Getting to Yes: Negotiating Agreement Without Giving In* (2nd edition). New York: Penguin Group, 1991.

Slide 9–28

Tips for Analysis

- Know the people engaged in the negotiation; learn who has the authority to make a deal.
- Know your and the other side's BATNA and interests.
- Conduct a SWOT analysis (*Strengths, Weaknesses, Opportunities, Threats*).

Source: Fisher, Roger, William Ury, and Bruce Patton, editor. *Getting to Yes: Negotiating Agreement Without Giving In* (2nd edition). New York: Penguin Group, 1991.

Slide 9–29

Step 2: Preparation

- Create strategies to work with different negotiation styles.
- Examine the other side's point of view (relationships and potential conflict).
- Decide how to communicate (phone, email, face-to-face, through third party).
- Exchange information.

Source: Fisher, Roger, William Ury, and Bruce Patton, editor. *Getting to Yes: Negotiating Agreement Without Giving In* (2nd edition). New York: Penguin Group, 1991.

Slide 9–30

Tips for Preparation

- Focus on how you will investigate options for mutual gain.
- Prepare objective criteria and standards to suggest for decision making.
- Match your strategy to the situation and style of participants.
- Plan with the idea that anything can happen.

Source: Fisher, Roger, William Ury, and Bruce Patton, editor. *Getting to Yes: Negotiating Agreement Without Giving In* (2nd edition). New York: Penguin Group, 1991.

Slide 9–31

Common Negotiation Styles

- Aggressive (or Confrontational): Indicates a strong need to control situations; described as persistent, domineering, decisive

- Assertive (or Persuasive): Indicates an approach using facts and logic to uphold position; described as determined, collaborative, persuasive

Source: Gosselin, Tom. *Practical Negotiating: Tools, Tactics and Techniques*. Hoboken, New Jersey: John Wiley and Sons, Inc., 2007.

Slide 9–32

Common Negotiation Styles

- Open (or Responsive): Indicates an open personality and good listening skills with a tendency to ask questions; described as flexible, approachable, understanding

- Avoiding (or Withdrawing): Indicates conflict avoidance and aversion to risk; described as cautious, compromising

Source: Gosselin, Tom. *Practical Negotiating: Tools, Tactics and Techniques*. Hoboken, New Jersey: John Wiley and Sons, Inc., 2007.

Slide 9–33

Criteria and Standards

- Focus on the "consistency principle": Appear reasonable and rational in making decisions.

- Beware of deferring to authority based strictly on status.

- Identify the other side's standards as legitimate and anticipate any arguments.

Source: Fisher, Roger, William Ury, and Bruce Patton, editor. *Getting to Yes: Negotiating Agreement Without Giving In* (2nd edition). New York: Penguin Group, 1991.

Slide 9–34

Criteria and Standards

Negotiations should involve:

- A wise agreement based on principles and interests.

- An efficient process for open communication.

- An improved relationship between the parties (or at minimum, a neutral one).

Source: Fisher, Roger, William Ury, and Bruce Patton, editor. *Getting to Yes: Negotiating Agreement Without Giving In* (2nd edition). New York: Penguin Group, 1991.

Slide 9–35

Step 3: Communication

- Explore differences and solutions.

- Use a variety of tactics to address negotiation styles.

- Develop rapport and build trust.

- Signal expectations and leverage.

- Probe first, then share information.

Source: Fisher, Roger, William Ury, and Bruce Patton, editor. *Getting to Yes: Negotiating Agreement without Giving In* (2nd edition). New York: Penguin Group, 1991.

Slide 9–36

Tips for Communication

- Pay attention to cultural differences in both verbal and nonverbal communication.

- Be sensitive to the mood or atmosphere during the discussion.

- Keep the people and the problem separate; avoid focusing on egos.

- Listen more and speak less.

Source: Fisher, Roger, William Ury, and Bruce Patton, editor. *Getting to Yes: Negotiating Agreement Without Giving In* (2nd edition). New York: Penguin Group, 1991.

Slide 9–37

Nonverbal Communication

- Be aware of your counterpart's nonverbal behaviors (i.e., gestures, tone of voice, posture, facial expression).

- Be aware of your own nonverbal behaviors and mood.

- Respond appropriately to the other side's nonverbal behaviors to be more receptive.

Slide 9–38

Leverage

If *Weak*:
- Appeal to counterpart's desire to minimize future risk.

- Appeal to counterpart's sympathy.

If *Strong*:
- Let the other side know your options (not that you'll exercise them all).

- Indicate your willingness to be flexible.

Source: Shell, G. Richard. *Bargaining for Advantage: Negotiation Strategies for Reasonable People.* New York: Penguin Group, 2006.

Slide 9–39

Step 4: Proposal

- Offer a solution to the issue (specific suggestions for action).

- Clarify roles to carry out the deal.

- Determine any deadlines and incremental steps.

- Decide a process for ongoing communication.

Source: Fisher, Roger, William Ury, and Bruce Patton, editor. *Getting to Yes: Negotiating Agreement Without Giving In* (2nd edition). New York: Penguin Group, 1991.

Slide 9–40

Tips for Proposal

- Base suggestions on uncovered interests and mutual gain.

- Be realistic and reasonable with deadlines and expectations.

- Engage others to determine next steps and processes.

- Match roles with individual strengths.

- Focus on achieving the primary goals of the negotiation.

Source: Fisher, Roger, William Ury, and Bruce Patton, editor. *Getting to Yes: Negotiating Agreement Without Giving In* (2nd edition). New York: Penguin Group, 1991.

Slide 9–41

Step 5: Commitment

- Secure *commitment*, not just agreement.

- Establish accountability to each other (i.e., what will be lost if either party fails to perform?).

- Gain signatures on a written agreement to bind the commitment.

Source: Fisher, Roger, William Ury, and Bruce Patton, editor. *Getting to Yes: Negotiating Agreement Without Giving In* (2nd edition). New York: Penguin Group, 1991.

Slide 9–42

Tips for Commitment

- Pay attention to social rituals (signs of respect and trust, such as a handshake).

- Consider making the commitment public through an announcement.

- Know what steps need to be taken to draft a legal contract.

- Complete a simultaneous exchange (i.e., a title or deed for payment).

Source: Fisher, Roger, William Ury, and Bruce Patton, editor. *Getting to Yes: Negotiating Agreement Without Giving In* (2nd edition). New York: Penguin Group, 1991.

Slide 9–43

Investigating Interests

Lisa J. Downs

American Society for Training & Development

Slide 9–44

Importance of Interests

- One of the most important aspects of effective negotiation is to identify shared interests with the other side.

- Each side in a negotiation has multiple interests; the key is to uncover them.

Slide 9–45

Importance of Interests

- Acknowledge the other party's interests as part of the issue; use these to look forward, not back.

- Be tough on the problem at hand but easy on the people; remember to focus on the issue, not on individual personalities.

Slide 9–46

Questions to Ask

To think about interests, ask…

- How do our interests compare to theirs (as we know them)?

- What can they give me that I need?

- What can I give them that they need?

- How can we each provide value?

- How can we make this process easier?

Slide 9–47

Creating Options

- Broaden your options rather than provide a single answer.

- Don't judge options and ideas; search for mutual benefit.

Slide 9–48

Creating Options

- Know your goals, and take those in with you to the negotiation.

- Set realistic objectives; know the facts about the deal and the other party.

Slide 9–49

Barriers to Creating Options

- Judging an idea prematurely
- Looking for one answer (a silver bullet)
- Assuming there's not enough to go around (only so many pieces in the pie)
- Thinking that the other side's problem is theirs to fix (no joint problem solving)

Slide 9–50

Brainstorming

- Brainstorming is a powerful way to create options without judgment.
- It can be done among colleagues or with participants from the other party.
- Focus on idea generation, rather than criticism or evaluation.

Slide 9–51

Brainstorming Tips

- Use a seating arrangement that allows people to see each other.
- Clarify the purpose of the brainstorming session.
- Capture everyone's ideas publicly and as accurately as possible.

Slide 9–52

Brainstorming Tips

- Highlight or prioritize the ideas to narrow the focus.
- Decide which ideas will help your negotiation the most.
- Clarify wording of these ideas and plan how they will be used.

Slide 9–53

Building Trust and Relationships

Lisa J. Downs

American Society for Training & Development

Slide 9–54

Trust in Negotiations

- The more the other party trusts you, the better the chances of reaching a mutually beneficial agreement.
- Characteristics such as dependability, honesty, and integrity are important when building trust.

Slide 9–55

Trust in Negotiations

Think about people you trust. What characteristics and behaviors do they exhibit that lead you to trust them?

Slide 9–56

Tips for Building Trust

- Be knowledgeable about the topics and issues involved in the negotiation.
- Follow through on commitments.
- Dress and behave in a professional manner.
- Be responsive to the other side's needs.
- Communicate well; listen.

Source: Stark, Peter B., and Jane Flaherty. *The Only Negotiating Guide You'll Ever Need: 101 Ways to Win Every Time in Any Situation.* New York: Broadway Books, 2003.

Slide 9–57

Tips for Building Trust

- Show genuine interest in their point of view.
- Ask good questions to probe for information and shared interests.
- Think in terms of abundance rather than scarcity (there's plenty for all).
- Use fair standards and criteria.

Source: Stark, Peter B., and Jane Flaherty. *The Only Negotiating Guide You'll Ever Need: 101 Ways to Win Every Time in Any Situation.* New York: Broadway Books, 2003.

Slide 9–58

Questioning Techniques

- Brainstorm questions to ask your counterpart before a negotiation conversation.
- Start with broad questions and adapt them as you go.
- To put your counterpart at ease, use appropriate small talk.

Source: Stark, Peter B., and Jane Flaherty. *The Only Negotiating Guide You'll Ever Need: 101 Ways to Win Every Time in Any Situation.* New York: Broadway Books, 2003.

Slide 9–59

Questioning Techniques

- Be sensitive to your counterpart's feelings and mood.
- Listen closely as the person answers your questions; avoid interruptions.
- Write down the responses; this will help capture information and show your counterpart respect.

Source: Stark, Peter B., and Jane Flaherty. *The Only Negotiating Guide You'll Ever Need: 101 Ways to Win Every Time in Any Situation.* New York: Broadway Books, 2003.

Slide 9–60

The Untrustworthy

Think about someone you do *not* trust. What are some ways you can protect yourself and your organization during negotiations with an untrustworthy person?

Slide 9–61

Their Point of View

- Prepare to negotiate from both your and the other side's point of view.

- Clarify the purpose of the negotiation for both sides.

- Arm yourself well with facts to boost trust and confidence.

Source: Stark, Peter B., and Jane Flaherty. *The Only Negotiating Guide You'll Ever Need: 101 Ways to Win Every Time in Any Situation.* New York: Broadway Books, 2003.

Slide 9–62

Their Point of View

To think about point of view, ask:
- What is the ideal outcome?
- What are all of the issues to be negotiated?
- What are the needs of my counterpart and of the customers we both serve?
- What strategy or tactics should I use?
- What are the styles of the negotiators?

Source: Stark, Peter B., and Jane Flaherty. *The Only Negotiating Guide You'll Ever Need: 101 Ways to Win Every Time in Any Situation.* New York: Broadway Books, 2003.

Slide 9–63

Negotiation Tactics

Lisa J. Downs

American Society for Training & Development

Slide 9–64

Common Tactics

- A variety of tactics, if used by either side in a negotiation, can help lead to mutually beneficial agreements.

- Each negotiation may require different tactics, depending on the parties and issues involved.

Slide 9–65

Common Tactics

- Packaging (Bundling): Combining two or more items to add value to a deal, such as price, terms, and quantity

- Framing: Positioning a solution in terms of a certain perspective, such as a gain versus a loss, or a positive versus a negative

Source: Gosselin, Tom. *Practical Negotiating: Tools, Tactics and Techniques.* Hoboken, New Jersey: John Wiley and Sons, Inc., 2007.

Slide 9–66

Common Tactics

- Balancing the Scales: Illustrating what each party gives and receives to demonstrate a fair deal

- Objective Criteria: Adding credibility by presenting data from an objective source

Source: Gosselin, Tom. *Practical Negotiating: Tools, Tactics and Techniques.* Hoboken, New Jersey: John Wiley and Sons, Inc., 2007.

Slide 9–67

Common Tactics

- Scaling: Asking the other side to rate the importance of an issue, that is, on a scale from 1 to 5

- Examining Possibilities (What If?): Investigating alternatives by assessing what the other party will consider

Source: Gosselin, Tom. *Practical Negotiating: Tools, Tactics and Techniques.* Hoboken, New Jersey: John Wiley and Sons, Inc., 2007.

Slide 9–68

Common Tactics

- Pleading Ignorance: Asking for further explanation to buy time and clarify the counterpart's position

- Patience: Waiting it out and not allowing yourself to be pushed into a decision; builds trust and disarms the other side

Source: Gosselin, Tom. *Practical Negotiating: Tools, Tactics and Techniques.* Hoboken, New Jersey: John Wiley and Sons, Inc., 2007.

Slide 9–69

Deciding on Tactics

Ask questions, such as these:

- What is the level of trust?
- What time constraints, if any, exist?
- How open is everyone to different outcomes?
- What outcome is desired?

Slide 9–70

Deciding on Tactics

- Think about the people involved and their styles.
- Anticipate the counterpart's behavior.
- Decide how to respond to anticipated behaviors.

Slide 9–71

Barriers to Negotiation

Lisa J. Downs

American Society for Training & Development

Slide 9–72

Common Barriers

- Many barriers exist that can hinder the progress of a negotiation and negatively affect its chances of success.

- These can include characteristics or the personalities of the parties involved and adversarial tactics.

Source: Watkins, Michael. *Negotiation.* Boston: Harvard Business School Press, 2003.

Slide 9–73

Common Barriers

- Communication Barriers: Examples include poor documentation of conversations, lack of dialogue, or bad listening behavior.

- Cultural or Gender Barriers: Examples include language difficulties, misunderstandings, or pace of work.

Source: Watkins, Michael. *Negotiation*. Boston: Harvard Business School Press, 2003.

Slide 9–74

Common Barriers

- Saboteur (Spoiler): A key stakeholder who tries to block the negotiation; can be an active or passive resistor.

- Lack of Trust: A weak relationship exists between the parties involved; tension or skepticism of reliability may be factors.

Source: Watkins, Michael. *Negotiation*. Boston: Harvard Business School Press, 2003.

Slide 9–75

Common Barriers

- Lack of Information: One or both sides fail to provide necessary information about issues, criteria, desired outcomes, or interests.

- Battle of Wills: A counterpart views each negotiation as a test of wills; could lead to bluffing or attempts to trip up the other side.

Source: Watkins, Michael. *Negotiation*. Boston: Harvard Business School Press, 2003.

Slide 9–76

Adversarial Tactics

- Anchoring: Putting the first offer on the table to establish a point of reference and gain a psychological advantage

- On the Clock: Setting an expiration date on an offer to pressure the other side to accept

Source: Watkins, Michael. *Negotiation*. Boston: Harvard Business School Press, 2003.

Slide 9–77

Adversarial Tactics

- Fait Accompli: Doing something that is irreversible without negotiating it first, that is, asking for forgiveness and not permission

- Good Guy/Bad Guy: In team negotiations, when one person pretends to be on your side whereas the other pretends to be tough and unreasonable

Source: Stark, Peter B., and Jane Flaherty. *The Only Negotiating Guide You'll Ever Need: 101 Ways to Win Every Time in Any Situation*. New York: Broadway Books, 2003.

Slide 9–78

Adversarial Tactics

- Bluffing: Lying or misrepresenting an issue or position to pressure the other side

- Funny Money: Breaking down sums of money into small parts (dollars and cents) to detract from the total cost

Source: Stark, Peter B., and Jane Flaherty. *The Only Negotiating Guide You'll Ever Need: 101 Ways to Win Every Time in Any Situation*. New York: Broadway Books, 2003.

Slide 9–79

Adversarial Tactics

- Take It or Leave It: Making a final offer by signaling that a limit has been reached; stating that this is a last offer

- Threats: Warning that there will be unpleasant consequences if the other side does not comply or accept a deal

Source: Stark, Peter B., and Jane Flaherty. *The Only Negotiating Guide You'll Ever Need: 101 Ways to Win Every Time in Any Situation*. New York: Broadway Books, 2003.

Slide 9–80

Overcoming Barriers

- Work through the planning process to understand all issues and people involved.

- Anticipate questions and problems the other side may have.

- Set clear expectations at the start.

- Use win-win tactics to counter tactics that are more adversarial.

Slide 9–81

Ethics in Negotiation

Lisa J. Downs

American Society for Training & Development

Slide 9–82

Role of Ethics

- Ethics and conduct are crucial parts of your identity.

- This will translate into how you behave in negotiations.

- The higher your ethical standards, the higher the cost you must be willing to pay in a negotiation so they are upheld.

Source: Shell, G. Richard. *Bargaining for Advantage: Negotiation Strategies for Reasonable People*. New York: Penguin Group, 2006.

Slide 9–83

Role of Ethics

- The lower your ethical standards, the greater the cost to your reputation.

- The lower the ethical standards of your counterpart, the more energy you'll need to spend to fight for your interests.

- Personal integrity is a key trait of a skilled negotiator.

Source: Shell, G. Richard. *Bargaining for Advantage: Negotiation Strategies for Reasonable People*. New York: Penguin Group, 2006.

Slide 9–84

Legal Issues

- Basic principles of fairness and prudence exist in bargaining conduct.

- Typically, negotiators act in "good faith" to produce the best deal for all.

- Laws around fraud focus on knowingly misrepresenting important facts on which the other side relies, which causes damage.

Source: Shell, G. Richard. *Bargaining for Advantage: Negotiation Strategies for Reasonable People*. New York: Penguin Group, 2006.

Slide 9–85

Approaches to Bargaining Ethics

- Poker Approach: Negotiation is a game with rules defined by law; conduct within the rules is ethical, but conduct outside the rules is not; deception is essential.
- Idealist Approach: The same ethics that apply at home should apply in negotiations; people must be held responsible and do the right thing.

Source: Shell, G. Richard. *Bargaining for Advantage: Negotiation Strategies for Reasonable People.* New York: Penguin Group, 2006.

Slide 9–86

Approaches to Bargaining Ethics

- Pragmatist Approach: Deception in bargaining may be necessary at times, but a practical solution is best; questionable tactics are wrong if they cost the negotiator more in the long run.

Which approach do you identify with most? Why?

Source: Shell, G. Richard. *Bargaining for Advantage: Negotiation Strategies for Reasonable People.* New York: Penguin Group, 2006.

Slide 9–87

Unethical Negotiators

- When the competition is tough, the risk of unethical behavior rises.
- Those with more power may abuse it by behaving unethically.
- When the stakes matter, and not the relationship between the parties, unethical behavior may result.

Slide 9–88

Guarding Against the Unethical

- Research the other party's background by checking sources and talking with others.
- Network to seek recommendations and referrals; ongoing relationships raise ethical standards.

Slide 9–89

Guarding Against the Unethical

- Insist on fairness and integrity.
- Keep your perspective and emotions in check.
- Maintain your high ethical standards by refusing to engage in unethical behavior.

Slide 9–90

Points to Remember

- Ethical issues are at the core of many bargaining situations; credibility is at stake.
- The best negotiators take their personal integrity very seriously.
- Strong personal values translate into better bargaining.

Slide 9–91

Negotiation Success Factors

Lisa J. Downs

American Society for Training &
Development

Slide 9–92

Defining Success

- It is important to have measures of success to know if your approach to negotiation is effective.

- Negotiating goals should be in alignment with those of the organization.

- Ask, "What does success look like?"

Slide 9–93

Success Factors

- BATNA: Has the deal been measured against the best alternative to a negotiated agreement?

- Relationship: Did the negotiation result in both parties being interested in working together again in the future?

Source: Watkins, Michael. *Negotiation*. Boston: Harvard Business School Press, 2003.

Slide 9–94

Success Factors

- Options: Have you looked for innovative and effective solutions with mutual benefit?

- Interests: Are all interests satisfied to an acceptable level as a result of the deal?

Source: Watkins, Michael. *Negotiation*. Boston: Harvard Business School Press, 2003.

Slide 9–95

Success Factors

- Criteria: Did we use objective, agreed-upon criteria to select an option?

- Communication: Did the negotiations create an environment of open, respectful communication?

Source: Watkins, Michael. *Negotiation*. Boston: Harvard Business School Press, 2003.

Slide 9–96

Success Factors

- Commitment: Is a realistic, workable plan in place, with agreement from all parties?

- Experience: Did the overall experience improve negotiation skills and lead to the desire to engage in future negotiations?

Source: Watkins, Michael. *Negotiation*. Boston: Harvard Business School Press, 2003.

Slide 9–97

Effective Negotiators

- Support the goals of the organization during the negotiation.
- Prepare before and during the negotiation process.
- Recognize potential obstacles and find ways around them.

Slide 9–98

Effective Negotiators

- Learn more about the other side's interests and issues during the negotiation.
- Help the other side investigate interests and approach issues with creativity.

Slide 9–99

Effective Negotiators

- Build relationships and earn support from others.
- Are trustworthy, ethical, and reliable.
- Keep the negotiation about the issues and not about the people.

Slide 9–100

Setting Negotiation Goals

- Always enter a negotiation situation with specific goals.
- Think about what you really want—what is most important.
- Set a realistic target.

Slide 9–101

Setting Negotiation Goals

- Be specific; use numbers and measures as much as possible.
- Commit to the goal by sharing it with others and making it available in printed form.
- Take the goal with you into negotiation conversations.

Slide 9–102

Keep in Mind...

- Continuous improvement and goal achievement can also be important negotiation success factors.
- Documenting and revisiting lessons learned will help with future negotiations.
- Clear expectations are the foundation for many negotiations.

Content Modules

- Detailed instructions on how to use the content modules
- Content Modules 10–1 through 10–11

This chapter contains all of the content modules referenced in the sample agendas in previous chapters. The term *content* refers to the emphases within the modules. Each content module is a self-contained learning experience that can be used either as a stand-alone training session or incorporated into a broader agenda. The interactive designs explore content areas in a step-by-step fashion. They are handy, readily available resources to help facilitators address the issues that learners face in negotiation skills training.

Using the Content Modules

These content modules are the building blocks of a training program for coaches. Each module includes, as appropriate:

- Step-by-step instructions
- Key learning points
- Discussion questions
- A list of materials to be used in each module, including
  - Training instruments
  - PowerPoint presentations
  - Structured exercises

Trainers should review the content module, along with all of the resources used in the module. After you have become familiar with the content, follow the step-by-step instructions to facilitate the module. Time estimates are provided for each module and each step, but the time needed for activities may vary, depending on the facilitators and the participants.

A trainer can modify these modules to comply with the organization's priorities; the readiness level of potential participants; or the resources in terms of time, space, and availability of trainees. These modules apply many of the principles of adult learning specified in chapter 3 of this book. The trainer should understand and be committed to these principles before he or she revises the step-by-step approaches included here.

The Modules

The modules included in this chapter emphasize how to learn through participation, using the materials in this book. As recommended in chapter 2, conduct a needs assessment before you decide which modules will be used, how they will be modified, and how you will combine various modules into longer sessions.

This section includes 11 modules:

◆ **Content Module 10–1: Participant Introductions.** To create a collaborative learning environment, this module introduces participants to each other and suggests that their roles are to contribute to the learning process.

◆ **Content Module 10–2: Types of Negotiations.** This module explains the two most common types of negotiations and the four most common outcomes of any negotiation conversation.

◆ **Content Module 10–3: Negotiation Self-Assessment.** This module helps participants assess their strengths and weaknesses in negotiation and explores how poor negotiation skills can negatively affect communications with others.

◆ **Content Module 10–4: Core Principles of Negotiation.** Negotiation principles such as BATNA (*Best Alternative To a Negotiated Agreement*), ZOPA (*Zone Of Possible Agreement*), and wants versus needs are explained in this module.

◆ **Content Module 10–5: Steps to Negotiating.** The five-step process for effective negotiation is included in this module.

- **Content Module 10–6: Investigating Interests.** This module helps participants understand and use techniques to discover the interests of a negotiation counterpart and incorporate them into a negotiation plan.

- **Content Module 10–7: Building Trust and Relationships.** Participants focus on how to look at another's point of view and learn how important it is to ask good questions as a tool to build trust.

- **Content Module 10–8: Negotiation Tactics.** This module identifies the many tactics used in negotiation, teaches participants how to recognize them, and gives them the opportunity to practice some of them.

- **Content Module 10–9: Barriers to Negotiation.** This module helps participants learn about various obstacles to negotiation situations and how to deal with them.

- **Content Module 10–10: Ethics in Negotiation.** Although often overlooked, ethical issues in negotiation and the critical role they play are examined in this module.

- **Content Module 10–11: Negotiation Success Factors.** The many factors for successful negotiation are reviewed in this module, which also includes a wrap-up activity to help participants focus on a negotiation success plan.

Content Module 10–1: Participant Introductions

To create a collaborative learning environment, this module introduces participants to each other and suggests that their roles are to contribute to the learning process.

TIME

- 10 minutes, and an additional 3 minutes for each participant

AGENDA

- Discuss key points. (5 minutes)

- Facilitate introduction exercise. (approximately 3 minutes per participant)

- Review some of the strengths and learning priorities of participants. (5 minutes)

KEY POINTS

- Everyone has strengths in negotiation and communication, and each person can contribute to the learning environment.

- One person's development needs are often another's strengths.

INTRODUCTION EXERCISE

Use a variety of introduction techniques based on the time available and the facilitator's preference. One good technique is to ask participants to share information about themselves with the other participants and identify what they have in common with each other. At the end of each person's introduction, ask participants to indicate by a show of hands who had at least one thing in common with another person regarding his or her negotiation skills. Then, from this group, ask for a volunteer or two to share the common items. Introductions should include this information:

- Name

- Area or function in which the participant works

◆ How long the participant has been in that role or with the same organization

◆ One thing that the participant does well when it comes to negotiation

◆ One thing that the participant would like to learn about being a more effective negotiator

Content Module 10–2: Types of Negotiations

This module explains the two most common types of negotiations and the four most common outcomes of any negotiation conversation.

 TIME

♦   1 hour, 30 minutes

MATERIALS

♦   Structured Experience 12–1: Negotiation Partners (chapter 12)

♦   Structured Experience 12–2: Negotiation Scenarios (chapter 12)

♦   PowerPoint presentation *Types of Negotiations.ppt* (in the online materials)

AGENDA

♦   Facilitate Structured Experience 12–1: Negotiation Partners. (30 minutes)

♦   Lead group through the first discussion question below. (5 minutes)

♦   Review PowerPoint presentation "Types of Negotiation." (20 minutes)

♦   Lead group through remaining discussion questions while you review the PowerPoint (questions 2–4 are embedded in the slide deck).

♦   Facilitate Structured Experience 12–2: Negotiation Scenarios. (30 minutes)

♦   Review key points. (5 minutes)

 *KEY POINTS*

♦   There are two main types of negotiation, Adversarial Negotiation (also called Positional Negotiation) and Interest-Based Negotiation (also called Principled Negotiation).

♦   Interest-Based Negotiation is preferred because of its focus on cooperation and maximum gain for both sides.

◆ We negotiate in many different situations, whether with family and friends or with colleagues at work in business-related scenarios.

◆ Four common negotiation outcomes are: Lose-Lose, Win-Lose, Win-Win, and No Result.

DISCUSSION QUESTIONS

1. What does negotiation mean to you?

2. What are your experiences or examples with Adversarial Negotiation?

3. What are your experiences or examples with Interest-Based Negotiation?

4. Is win-win really possible? Can both sides get everything they want? Don't some trade-offs need to be made?

Content Module 10–3: Negotiation Self-Assessment

This module helps participants assess their strengths and weaknesses when it comes to negotiation and explores how poor negotiation can negatively affect communication with others.

TIME

+ 1 hour

MATERIALS

+ Assessment 11–2: Negotiation Self-Assessment (chapter 11)

AGENDA

+ Discuss key points. (5 minutes)

+ Administer the assessment and have participants review the section called "Why These Behaviors Are Important." (15 minutes)

+ Ask participants to divide into pairs and help each other complete the "Plan for Self-Improvement" at the end of the assessment. (20 minutes)

+ Lead entire group through discussion questions. (20 minutes)

KEY POINTS

+ Effective negotiators have clearly defined behaviors and are able to focus on issues rather than personalities, concentrate on building relationships, and seek common ground with their negotiation counterparts.

+ It's important to identify which negotiation behaviors are important to your interactions with others and to practice these behaviors.

+ Know your negotiation strengths and weaknesses to become a better negotiator.

DISCUSSION QUESTIONS

1. How can the strengths you identified in the self-assessment help you be an effective negotiator? (Ask for examples from past experiences.)

2. What can you do specifically to improve the areas identified in your self-assessment?

Content Module 10–4: Core Principles of Negotiation

Negotiation principles such as BATNA (*Best Alternative To a Negotiated Agreement*), ZOPA (*Zone Of Possible Agreement*), and wants versus needs are explained in this module.

TIME

◆   1 hour, 30 minutes

MATERIALS

◆   Structured Experience 12–3: BATNA Basics (chapter 12)

◆   PowerPoint presentation *Core Principles of Negotiation.ppt* (in the on-line materials)

AGENDA

◆   Lead group through discussion question 1. (5 minutes)

◆   Review PowerPoint presentation "Core Principles of Negotiation." (25 minutes)

◆   Tell the participants that they will get some time to practice creating a BATNA so they feel comfortable applying this principle.

◆   Facilitate Structured Experience 12–3: BATNA Basics. (45 minutes)

◆   Review the key points. Lead participants through the remaining discussion questions. (15 minutes)

KEY POINTS

◆   There are four core principles at play in negotiation: BATNA (*Best Alternative To a Negotiated Agreement*), ZOPA (*Zone Of Possible Agreement*), analyzing needs versus wants, and use of empathy.

◆   During negotiation, it is important to pay attention to someone's *explicit* needs (ones that are stated) and *implicit* needs (those implied by emotions).

◆   Use empathy (understand a counterpart's perspective, interests, and goals) to lead to better trust and joint problem-solving.

◆ Four common principles of influence can be factors during negotiations: reciprocity, social proof, liking, and scarcity. The ability to recognize when these principles are being used and how to navigate around them are good skills to help you negotiate a mutually beneficial agreement.

DISCUSSION QUESTIONS

1. Think of your most common negotiation situations. Do you typically know your bottom line when you enter any negotiation? Are you always clear about the circumstances in which you'd walk away?

2. What is an example of a situation in which you've used empathy during negotiation?

3. What techniques have you used to help distinguish between what someone wants and what they really need for a deal to work?

4. What is an example of a situation in which you've either experienced or used one of the four principles of influence in a negotiation?

Content Module 10–5: Steps to Negotiating

The five-step process for effective negotiation is included in this module.

TIME

- ◆ 2 hours, 15 minutes

MATERIALS

- ◆ Assessment 11–7: Nonverbal Communication Self-Assessment (chapter 11)

- ◆ Handout 12–1: Nonverbal Communication Chart (chapter 12)

- ◆ Training Instrument 11–1: Negotiation Conversation Preparation Sheet (chapter 11)

- ◆ Structured Experience 12–4: Nonverbal Negotiation (chapter 12)

- ◆ Structured Experience 12–5: Preparation Practice (chapter 12)

- ◆ PowerPoint presentation *Steps to Negotiating.ppt* (in the online materials)

AGENDA

- ◆ Lead group through Discussion Question 1. (5 minutes)

- ◆ Review slides 1–13 in PowerPoint presentation "Steps to Negotiating." (20 minutes)

- ◆ Administer Assessment 11–7 and ask participants to share their insights about their nonverbal communication and how this relates to their negotiation style. (15 minutes)

- ◆ Facilitate Structured Experience 12–4: Nonverbal Negotiation. (45 minutes)

- ◆ Review remaining slides in PowerPoint presentation "Steps to Negotiating." (10 minutes)

◆ Discuss the key points. Lead participants through the remaining discussion questions. (10 minutes)

◆ Facilitate Structured Experience 12–5: Preparation Practice. (30 minutes)

KEY POINTS

◆ Negotiation is a five-step process that includes everything from analysis and preparation to presentation of formal proposals.

◆ A variety of communication styles can surface during negotiation, and the negotiator must make a conscious effort to adapt to these styles as much as possible.

◆ To prepare ourselves to have a successful negotiation outcome, we must know in advance the leverage we can use if necessary.

◆ A clear commitment, preferably in writing, helps to hold each party in a negotiation responsible for the terms outlined in an agreement.

DISCUSSION QUESTIONS

1. What are some benefits of following a process for negotiation?

2. What is an example of a situation in which you encountered someone with a different communication style than yours during negotiations? What was the outcome?

3. Why is it important to get a firm commitment from a negotiation counterpart?

Content Module 10–6: Investigating Interests

This module helps participants understand and use techniques to discover the interests of a negotiation counterpart and incorporate them into a negotiation plan.

TIME

- ◆   1 hour, 15 minutes

MATERIALS

- ◆   Training Instrument 11–2: Brainstorming Checklist (chapter 11)

- ◆   Structured Experience 12–6: Brainstorming Best Practices (chapter 12)

- ◆   PowerPoint presentation *Investigating Interests.ppt* (in the online materials)

AGENDA

- ◆   Review PowerPoint presentation "Investigating Interests." (15 minutes)

- ◆   Facilitate Structured Experience 12-6: Brainstorming Best Practices. (45 minutes)

- ◆   Discuss the key points. Lead the participants through the discussion questions. (15 minutes)

KEY POINTS

- ◆   It's crucial to uncover common interests when you seek a win-win negotiation outcome.

- ◆   Ask a number of questions before you investigate interests with a negotiation counterpart, such as how you can meet the needs of both sides and what value each party can gain from the negotiation.

- ◆   Brainstorming is an effective technique to uncover interests.

- ◆   Two common barriers to successful investigation of interests are to judge ideas and have a mentality of scarcity.

DISCUSSION QUESTIONS

1. What is a situation in which you successfully uncovered the interests of a negotiation counterpart? How did this affect the outcome?

2. What techniques beyond brainstorming have you used to generate ideas and gain common ground during a negotiation?

3. When have you encountered a barrier to joint problem-solving during negotiation?

Content Module 10–7: Building Trust and Relationships

Participants focus on how to look at another's point of view and learn how important it is to ask good questions as a tool to build trust.

TIME

◆ 2 hours

MATERIALS

◆ Structured Experience 12–7: Out of the Question (chapter 12)

◆ Structured Experience 12–8: A Different Point of View (chapter 12)

◆ PowerPoint presentation *Building Trust and Relationships.ppt* (in the online materials)

AGENDA

◆ Review slides 1–7 in the PowerPoint presentation "Building Trust and Relationships," and ask the first discussion question below, which is imbedded in the slide deck. (15 minutes)

◆ Facilitate Structured Experience 12–7: Out of the Question. (40 minutes)

◆ Review remaining slides in PowerPoint presentation "Building Trust and Relationships," and ask the second discussion question below, which is imbedded in the slide deck. (10 minutes)

◆ Facilitate Structured Experience 12–8: A Different Point of View. (45 minutes)

◆ Discuss key points. Lead the group through the remaining discussion questions. (10 minutes)

KEY POINTS

◆ The more both sides in a negotiation trust each other, the better the outcome and strength of the negotiated agreement.

◆ Exhibit trustworthy behaviors: Listen well, follow through on commitments, and show genuine interest in the other side's needs.

- It's a good idea to brainstorm a list of questions to ask in a negotiation to indicate that you want to build a good relationship and commit to a mutually beneficial agreement.

- In any negotiation, consider each side's point of view to build trust and rapport.

DISCUSSION QUESTIONS

1. Think about people you trust. What characteristics and behaviors do they exhibit that lead you to trust them?

2. Think about someone you do not trust. What are some ways you can protect yourself and your organization during negotiation with an untrustworthy person?

3. What is an example of a situation in which you tried to build rapport with someone in a negotiation and failed? How did this affect the outcome?

4. What are some of the effects you've seen on negotiations with both strong and weak relationships?

Content Module 10–8: Negotiation Tactics

This module identifies the many tactics used in negotiation, teaches participants how to recognize them, and gives participants the opportunity to practice some of them.

TIME

* 1 hour

MATERIALS

* Handout 12–2: Common Negotiation Tactics

* Structured Experience 12–9: Tactics Testing (chapter 12)

* PowerPoint presentation *Negotiation Tactics.ppt* (in the online materials)

AGENDA

* Facilitate Structured Experience 12–9: Tactics Testing. (40 minutes)

* Review PowerPoint presentation "Negotiation Tactics." (10 minutes)

* Discuss the key points. Lead the participants through the discussion questions. (10 minutes)

KEY POINTS

* Many types of tactics are used in negotiation; consider the issues and people involved before you decide which ones to use.

* Some of the most common tactics used in negotiations include Framing, Balancing the Scales, and Pleading Ignorance.

* Gauge the level of trust in the negotiation relationship and assess the desired outcome before you use any tactics.

* To improve your negotiation skills, be ready to use some tactics, when appropriate, to move negotiations forward.

DISCUSSION QUESTIONS

1. Think about someone you know whom you consider to be a good negotiator. What tactics does he or she use?

2. What was a specific occasion in which you consciously used a negotiation tactic? How did it affect the outcome?

3. What specifically could you do to familiarize yourself with negotiation tactics that you think could lead to win-win outcomes?

Content Module 10–9: Barriers to Negotiation

This module helps participants learn about various obstacles to negotiation situations and how to deal with them.

TIME

◆ 1 hour, 15 minutes

MATERIALS

◆ Handout 12–3: Barrier Role-Play Scenarios

◆ Structured Experience 12–10: Beyond the Barriers (chapter 12)

◆ PowerPoint presentation *Barriers to Negotiation.ppt* (in the online materials)

AGENDA

◆ Lead group through the first discussion question below. (5 minutes)

◆ Review PowerPoint presentation "Barriers to Negotiation." (15 minutes)

◆ Facilitate Structured Experience 12–10: Beyond the Barriers. (45 minutes)

◆ Discuss the key points. Lead the participants through the remaining discussion questions. (10 minutes)

KEY POINTS

◆ A number of barriers can interfere with a successful negotiation outcome, including adversarial tactics and the personality of those involved.

◆ These barriers can involve issues with communication, culture, or indicate a lack of trust in the relationship.

◆ Some of the most common adversarial tactics that can be used in negotiations include Fait Accompli, Good Guy/Bad Guy, Bluffing, and Take It or Leave It.

◆ To overcome barriers, it is good to have a clear process and to set expectations upfront with both parties, as well as anticipate each side's questions.

DISCUSSION QUESTIONS

1. Have you ever been involved in a negotiation where there were obvious barriers to reaching an agreement? If so, what was the experience like?

2. What is an example of a situation in which someone tried to use an adversarial tactic on you? How did you react? How did it feel?

3. What immediate concerns do you have about the ways to overcome barriers during negotiation?

4. What are some strategies you could use to overcome barriers that we haven't already discussed?

Content Module 10–10: Ethics in Negotiation

Although often overlooked, ethical issues in negotiation and the critical role they play are examined in this module.

TIME

◆ 1 hour, 30 minutes

MATERIALS

◆ Handout 12–4: Ethics Case Study for all participants

◆ Structured Experience 12–11: Examining Ethics (chapter 12)

◆ PowerPoint presentation *Ethics in Negotiation.ppt* (in the online materials)

AGENDA

◆ Review PowerPoint Presentation "Ethics in Negotiation," and ask participants the first discussion question below, which is embedded in the slide deck. (15 minutes)

◆ Facilitate Structured Experience 12–11: Examining Ethics. (60 minutes)

◆ Discuss the key points. Lead the participants through the remaining discussion questions. (15 minutes)

KEY POINTS

◆ Key traits of skilled negotiators are personal integrity and high ethical standards.

◆ Both sides in a negotiation typically act on good faith to create the best agreement for each party; unfortunately, fraud does occasionally occur.

◆ Three main approaches to ethics in negotiations are Poker, Idealist, and Pragmatist.

◆ Check the other party's background and stick to your values to help guard against others' possible unethical behavior.

DISCUSSION QUESTIONS

1. Which approach to negotiation ethics do you identify with most? Why?

2. Have you heard of this approach before? If so, from what source? If not, how does this change your view of negotiation?

3. Think back to a situation in which you encountered someone with questionable negotiation ethics. What specifically would you do to address the situation now?

4. Why would some people resort to unethical negotiation practices? What can you do to coach others on their negotiation ethics?

Content Module 10–11: Negotiation Success Factors

The many factors for successful negotiation are reviewed in this module, which also includes a wrap-up activity to help participants focus on a negotiation success plan.

TIME

- 1 hour, 15 minutes

MATERIALS

- Training Instrument 11–3: Negotiation Success Plan

- Structured Experience 12–12: What a Success! (chapter 12)

- PowerPoint presentation *Negotiation Success Factors.ppt* (in the online materials)

AGENDA

- Review PowerPoint presentation: "Negotiation Success Factors." (20 minutes)

- Discuss the key points. Lead the participants through the discussion questions. (10 minutes)

- Facilitate Structured Experience 12–12: What a Success! (45 minutes)

KEY POINTS

- Know in advance specific measures of success for a negotiation to help achieve the desired outcome and evaluate future negotiations.

- Look at items such as the BATNA, relationship, interests, and commitment; they can be key indicators of success during negotiation.

- Effective negotiators take the necessary time to prepare and focus on how to build relationships; they must learn about common interests and not allow personalities to get in the way.

- It's always a good idea to walk into a negotiation with a specific and realistic goal.

DISCUSSION QUESTIONS

1. What is an example of a situation in which you weren't sure what success looked like for a negotiation? What was the effect on the outcome?

2. Which success factors occur repeatedly for you in negotiation situations?

3. How can you encourage others to decide measures of success before a negotiation?

4. How will you set expectations with the other side for your next negotiation?

◆

Assessments and Training Instruments

What's in This Chapter?

- ◆ Instructions for using assessments and instruments
- ◆ Assessments 11–1 through 11–7
- ◆ Training Instruments 11–1 through 11–4

Many worksheets and data-gathering instruments are available to the facilitator of an effective negotiation skills training program. This chapter includes assessments and training instruments that rate relevant traits, competencies, and practices, as well as other tools to assist in the learning process.

An assessment differs from a test because the responses to the questions in an assessment are not considered right or wrong. Most of the assessments are designed to increase self-awareness; this process helps participants focus on learning objectives to which they can willingly commit.

Please note that we have included these training instruments for their usefulness, not for their predictive power. They have not been tested for reliability or validity, but they were designed primarily to generate data for action planning and personal commitment, as well as to promote learning about what is important. Participants can use some of the training instruments during the actual learning process.

Assessments and Training Instruments

- **Assessment 11–1: Learning Needs-Assessment Sheet.** Use this assessment during an interview with stakeholders in the organization to help assess the needs of learners and the client organization.

- **Assessment 11–2: Negotiation Self-Assessment.** This self-assessment helps participants understand and rate themselves on the competencies required to be a good negotiator. It also helps them focus on areas for improvement during training.

- **Assessment 11–3: Needs-Assessment Discussion Form.** Participants use this form to gather their thoughts and provide information for the facilitator in a needs-assessment focus group session.

- **Assessment 11–4: Facilitator Competencies.** Used as a self-assessment or as a follow-up questionnaire, this form helps establish learning priorities for your own development as a workshop facilitator. You may use it to solicit feedback from trainees after the session or at a later time.

- **Assessment 11–5: Negotiation Skills Follow-Up Assessment.** This survey is designed to learn how participants changed negotiation behaviors after their training. It is best to wait three to six months after the training before you conduct this type of assessment.

- **Assessment 11–6: Training Evaluation.** Use this form to conduct a Level 1 Smile Sheet evaluation. It allows training participants to provide reaction feedback for the workshop and the facilitator.

- **Assessment 11–7: Nonverbal Communication Self-Assessment.** The results of this self-assessment will help participants review and interpret the nonverbal feedback they typically send.

- **Training Instrument 11–1: Negotiation Conversation Preparation Sheet.** Used during Structured Experience 12–5 (Preparation Practice), this form helps participants through the planning stage of the negotiation process. It asks them to examine the desired outcome for the negotiation, as well as the interests and needs of both parties.

- **Training Instrument 11–2: Brainstorming Checklist.** Used in Structured Experience 12–6 (Brainstorming Best Practices), this checklist helps participants determine whether the group followed brainstorming guidelines, as an important aspect of investigating interests in negotiations.

- **Training Instrument 11–3: Negotiation Success Plan.** Used in Structured Experience 12–12, (Negotiation Success Planning), the worksheet helps participants evaluate how they can best achieve a successful outcome, as well as how they will address various success factors in the negotiation.

- **Training Instrument 11–4: Facilitation Preparation Checklist.** This tool helps the facilitator prepare for a training session and ensures that he or she has all of the materials and equipment necessary to conduct a workshop.

Assessment 11–1
Learning Needs-Assessment Sheet

Instructions: During interviews with stakeholders in the client organization, use this form to take notes to assess the needs of both learners and the organization itself. Be sure to understand the participant's response to each question before you write a summary of what he or she says. Assure the interviewee that the responses will be both anonymous and confidential.

1. How do you define negotiation?

2. How would you assess your own negotiation skills?

3. In your role in the organization, how would you benefit from negotiation skills training?

4. Would negotiation skills training benefit the organization at this time? Why or why not?

5. How would you assess the negotiation skills of others in the organization?

6. What specific behaviors have you observed that affect negotiation and should be addressed in a negotiation skills course?

7. What preferences do you have about how you might receive negotiation skills training?

8. Are others in the organization interested in receiving negotiation skills training?

9. Should all employees in the organization receive negotiation skills training, or should only select groups at a certain level receive training? Why?

10. How should negotiation skills training be marketed internally to draw attendees?

11. What results you would like to see for the organization after negotiation skills training?

12. What else can you tell me about your training needs at this time?

13. What other factors for success could affect negotiation skills training?

14. What questions do you have for me?

End the interview by thanking the participant for his or her candid responses to your questions. Reassure the interviewee that he or she will not be quoted by name, but the comments will be combined with others' responses to analyze common themes. Explain that the negotiation skills training will reflect the priorities of those interviewed.

Assessment 11–2
Negotiation Self-Assessment

Instructions: The purpose of this activity is to help you determine what you need to be a good negotiator and create an action plan for self-improvement in your negotiation skills. Place a ✓ in one of the boxes to the right of each item, depending on how you see yourself today. No one will see your ratings unless you share them, so please be honest with yourself.

NEGOTIATION BEHAVIOR	ALWAYS	FREQUENTLY	SOMETIMES	RARELY	NEVER
During negotiation, I...					
1. Focus on issues, not on personalities.	☐	☐	☐	☐	☐
2. Concentrate on relationship-building.	☐	☐	☐	☐	☐
3. Anticipate the interests of my counterpart.	☐	☐	☐	☐	☐
4. Avoid direct eye contact when I speak.	☐	☐	☐	☐	☐
5. Work to expose underlying motivations.	☐	☐	☐	☐	☐
6. Seek a win-win solution as much as possible.	☐	☐	☐	☐	☐
7. Offer solutions focused on my needs.	☐	☐	☐	☐	☐
8. Maintain my professionalism at all times.	☐	☐	☐	☐	☐
9. Take the necessary time to plan and prepare.	☐	☐	☐	☐	☐
10. Listen without judgment or criticism.	☐	☐	☐	☐	☐
11. Interrupt my counterpart to get my point across.	☐	☐	☐	☐	☐
12. Interject issues unrelated to the topic.	☐	☐	☐	☐	☐
13. Use nonverbal communication that is inconsistent with my words.	☐	☐	☐	☐	☐
14. Know my bottom line and when to walk out.	☐	☐	☐	☐	☐
15. Ask many questions to get needed information.	☐	☐	☐	☐	☐
16. Focus on finding common ground.	☐	☐	☐	☐	☐

continued on next page

Assessment 11–2, continued
Negotiation Self-Assessment

NEGOTIATION BEHAVIOR	ALWAYS	FREQUENTLY	SOMETIMES	RARELY	NEVER
17. Consider my counterpart's point of view.	☐	☐	☐	☐	☐
18. Adapt my tactics to my counterpart's style.	☐	☐	☐	☐	☐
19. React emotionally when I disagree.	☐	☐	☐	☐	☐
20. Use brainstorming or other techniques to investigate my counterpart's interests.	☐	☐	☐	☐	☐
21. Know which tactics will counteract those used by the other side.	☐	☐	☐	☐	☐
22. Think clearly in high-pressure situations.	☐	☐	☐	☐	☐
23. Gain a clear written commitment from my counterpart with actions and dates.	☐	☐	☐	☐	☐
24. Enjoy winning arguments and getting concessions.	☐	☐	☐	☐	☐
25. Create a nonthreatening environment.	☐	☐	☐	☐	☐

Analysis: If you responded "always," "frequently," or "sometimes" for items 4, 7, 11, 12, 13, 19, or 24, these may be areas in which you need to improve your negotiation skills, especially your interpersonal communication skills and willingness to seek a mutually beneficial agreement. You may also wish to address any of the remaining statements if you responded with "sometimes," "rarely," or "never," particularly for items 1, 6, 8, 15, 17, 20, and 25, which directly relate to effectively understanding a counterpart's needs and building trust and respect during a negotiation conversation.

Study this information and the following pages to see why those 25 behaviors are important to be a good negotiator. Then outline an action plan for self-improvement on the last page. Make sure it is a realistic plan to which you can fully commit yourself.

Why These Behaviors Are Important

The 25 behaviors represent areas you may need to address to become a more effective negotiator. They are of particular importance if you would like to improve your

continued on next page

negotiation skills; some of the behaviors, both negative and positive, may warrant additional attention.

- **Focus on issues, not on personalities.** If you focus more on the people involved in a negotiation, or have preconceived ideas about how someone's personality will affect the outcome, you may completely miss the underlying issues involved in a negotiation.

- **Concentrate on relationship-building.** A solid relationship with your counterpart that is built on trust is important to good negotiation. This will lead to mutually beneficial agreements and increase the chance that you will be able to work together for a common goal in the future.

- **Anticipate the interests of my counterpart.** It is helpful to know your counterpart's possible interests before you negotiate a deal. Armed with this information, you will be able to enter a conversation ready to discuss your common interests and will reach an agreement more quickly and easily.

- **Work to expose underlying motivations.** When you uncover the other side's needs, wants, motivations, and interests during negotiation, it helps build a strong relationship, as well as signals that you want to work toward a win-win solution.

- **Seek a win-win solution as much as possible.** Although a solution that is truly a win for both sides may not always be possible, this is usually the goal of many negotiations. This approach can lead to conversations that are less adversarial and more productive.

- **Take the necessary time to plan and prepare.** Good preparation before any negotiation conversation is essential to focus on key issues and the underlying interests of both parties to reach agreement. Without necessary background information, it can be difficult to address everyone's needs.

- **Listen without judgment or criticism.** To be an effective negotiator, it is important to consider your counterpart's views without judgment or criticism. Otherwise, the focus may shift to personalities and away from issues, which could harm your relationship and interfere with your negotiation.

- **Interrupt my counterpart to get my point across.** Sometimes we are so concerned with our own comments, opinions, or responses that we interrupt others. Make a conscious effort not to interrupt when someone else speaks; it will greatly enhance your ability to listen, as well as help your counterpart communicate his or her thoughts more effectively.

- **Interject issues unrelated to the topic.** Don't mention or think about other issues unrelated to the topic at hand during negotiation conversations. This behavior can inhibit your ability to listen and prevent you from being taken seriously, which can make you misunderstand or miss vital information. It can also send a signal that you are not sensitive to your counterpart's interests.

continued on next page

Assessment 11–2, continued
Negotiation Self-Assessment

◆ **Use nonverbal communication that is inconsistent with my words.** Facial expressions, tone of voice, gestures, and posture that contradict your statements may make it more difficult for others to read your emotions effectively and respond accordingly. This could alienate your counterpart and possibly breed distrust.

◆ **Know my bottom line and when to walk out.** In some negotiations you may be unable to reach a deal, which could be the best solution in certain situations. It is therefore most effective to know the conditions that would cause you to walk away and whether there are any nonnegotiable items for your organization.

◆ **Adapt my tactics to my counterpart's style.** This is important to help ensure that you consider the other side's approach to a negotiation; such efforts help build relationships but do not compromise your interests and needs.

◆ **React emotionally when I disagree.** A counterpart may find this behavior offensive and may be unwilling to share information or explore common interests with a negotiator in the future. This would affect the relationship between both parties and interfere with understanding the other side's message or view.

◆ **Gain a clear written commitment from my counterpart with actions and dates.** A clear, solid action plan with specific deadlines and deliverables ensures that a mutually beneficial agreement will move forward with an agreed-upon outcome. It also helps both sides accept responsibility for results.

◆ **Create a nonthreatening environment.** A relaxing environment encourages others to share information; it also helps negotiators focus on their counterparts and be more open to what is said by the other party. This establishes a positive relationship and leads to greater problem-solving and investigating interests.

continued on next page

Assessment 11–2, continued
Negotiation Self-Assessment

Plan for Self-Improvement

1. Which two or three negotiation behaviors need the most improvement?

   _____

   _____

2. What steps can you take to improve these behaviors?

   _____

   _____

3. What are the first two or three steps you will take?

   _____

   _____

4. How will you measure your results to determine whether you have improved your negotiation skills?

   _____

   _____

5. How will you personally benefit from improved negotiation skills?

   _____

   _____

6. What support do you need from others that will help you improve?

   _____

   _____

7. Who needs to know about your efforts to improve your negotiation skills?

   _____

   _____

8. How will you share this information with him or her?

   _____

   _____

continued on next page

Assessment 11–2, continued
Negotiation Self-Assessment

9. Which behaviors are particularly important for your work life? Which are important for your home life?

_____

_____

10. By what date would you like to see noticeable improvement in your negotiation skills?

_____

_____

Assessment 11–3
Needs-Assessment Discussion Form

Instructions: Use this sheet to prepare your comments for the focus group discussion. Write the first thoughts that come to mind in response to each question. You may make any changes to your responses that you like as the discussion progresses. Please do not write your name on this form. The facilitator will collect the form at the conclusion of the session.

1. How would you describe the negotiation skills of people in the organization?

2. What behaviors have you observed when others negotiate with you?

3. What level(s) of employees do you think would benefit from negotiation skills training? Why?

4. How receptive would you be to training to improve your own negotiation skills?

5. How receptive do you think others in the organization would be to negotiation skills training?

6. What challenges or roadblocks may be present in the organization that could affect the success of a negotiation skills training session?

7. What would you personally like to see included in a negotiation skills training session?

8. How would you prefer that training be offered to you? (circle one)

    a. Private, individual instruction

    b. Half-day group session

    c. One-day group session

    d. One and a half-day to two-day group session

    e. No preference

Thank you for your cooperation in this needs assessment.

Assessment 11–4
Facilitator Competencies

This assessment instrument will help you manage your own professional development and increase the effectiveness of your negotiation skills training sessions. Training facilitators can use this instrument in several ways:

◆ **Self-assessment.** Use the assessment to rate yourself on the five-point scale to generate an overall profile and help determine the competency areas that you most need to improve.

◆ **End-of-course feedback.** Honest feedback from the training participants can lessen the possibility that facilitators deceive themselves regarding the 12 competencies. Trainees may not be able to rate the facilitator on all 12, so it may be necessary to ask the participants to rate only those that they feel qualified to evaluate accurately.

◆ **Observer feedback.** Facilitators may observe each other's training sessions and provide highly useful information on the 12 competencies that are crucial to conduct effective negotiation skills training.

◆ **Repeat ratings.** This assessment can be used to track professional growth on the competencies needed to be an effective facilitator. The repeat measure may be obtained as often as needed to gauge progress on action plans for improvement.

The Competencies

Facilitators face many challenges whenever they lead a training session. The facilitator must be effective at many things to ensure that he or she meets the participants' learning needs and that the organization achieves its desired results for the training. This assessment contains a set of 12 important competencies that are required for effective negotiation skills training. Not all seasoned facilitators have expertise in all of these competencies, but they may represent learning and growth areas for almost any facilitator.

Here is a detailed explanation of the importance of each of the dozen crucial elements of facilitator competence:

1. **Understanding adult learners.** Uses knowledge of the principles of adult learning to design and deliver training.

   Effective facilitators are able to draw on the experiences of the learners in a training session; they must provide them with content and tools that they can immediately apply to engage them fully and help them see the value of the learning. It's also important to address the participants' various learning styles, as well as to give them opportunities to solve problems and think critically so they can work through real business issues and develop additional skills.

continued on next page

Assessment 11–4, *continued*
Facilitator Competencies

2. **Presentation skills.** Presents content clearly to achieve the desired outcomes of the training. Encourages learners to lead group discussions effectively and generate their own answers.

   Of all the competencies a facilitator uses during a training session, none may be more obvious than the need to have exceptional presentation skills. The facilitator's ability to present content effectively and in an entertaining way is one of the first things learners notice and is a large part of a successful workshop. The nature of adult learning makes it equally important for the facilitator to be able to initiate, draw out, guide, and summarize information gleaned from large-group discussions during a training session. The facilitator's role is not to feed answers to learners as if they are empty vessels waiting to be filled. Rather, the facilitator's primary task is to generate learning on the part of the participants through their own process of discovery.

3. **Communication skills.** Expresses self well, verbally and in writing. Understands non-verbal communication and listens effectively.

   The facilitator must be able to do more than present information and lead discussions; it is vital for a facilitator to be highly skilled in all aspects of communication. A facilitator should use language that learners can understand; give clear directions for activities; involve trainees through appropriate humor, anecdotes, and examples; and build on the ideas of others to ensure that training sessions are engaging and highly valuable for the participants. It's also important to listen well and attend to learners' nonverbal communication to create common meaning and mutual understanding.

4. **Emotional intelligence.** Respects learners' viewpoints, knowledge, and experience. Recognizes and responds appropriately to others' feelings, attitudes, and concerns.

   Learners of many different backgrounds, experience levels, and opinions may be in the same training sessions, so facilitators must be able to handle a variety of situations and conversations well and also be sensitive to others' emotions. They must pay close attention to the dynamics in the room, be flexible enough to make immediate changes to activities during training to meet the needs of learners, and create an open and trusting learning environment. Attendees should be able to express their opinions, ask questions, and participate in activities without fear of repercussion or disapproval. Learners' emotions may be monitored during a training session to help the facilitator gauge when to change gears if conflict arises, whether discussion needs to be refocused on desired outcomes, or whether there is a need to delve deeper into a topic to encourage further learning.

continued on next page

Assessment 11–4, continued

Facilitator Competencies

5. **Training methods.** Varies instructional approaches to address different learning styles and hold learners' interest.

All trainees have preferred learning styles, and one of the keys to effective training facilitation is to use a variety of methods to address them. Some people are more visual ("see it") learners, and others are more auditory ("hear it") or kinesthetic ("do it") learners. An effective facilitator should be familiar with a variety of training methods to tap into each participant's style(s) and maintain interest during the training session. These methods may include activities such as small-group activities, individual exercises, case studies, role plays, simulations, and games.

6. **Subject matter expertise.** Possesses deep knowledge of training content and applicable experience to draw upon.

Facilitators must have solid background knowledge of the training topic at hand and be able to share related experience to help learners connect theory to real-world scenarios. Anecdotes and other examples that illustrate how the training content relates to participants' circumstances and work enhance the learning experience and encourage learners to apply the information and use the tools they have been given. Facilitators must know their topics inside and out so they can answer trainees' questions and guide them toward problem-solving and skill development.

7. **Questioning skills.** Asks questions in a way that stimulates learners' understanding and curiosity, and encourages critical thinking.

An effective questioning technique works well to assess learners' understanding of training content, as well as provides opportunities for them to analyze information and think critically. When learners ask questions, the facilitator can see where there may be confusion or a need to go over concepts again for better understanding. Similarly, when a facilitator asks thought-provoking questions in a way that invites participation, learners can brainstorm solutions to problems; they can also think through situations to help them apply the training content to the issues they deal with on a regular basis.

8. **Eliciting behavior change.** Influences others effectively both individually and within groups. Gains support and commitment from others to achieve common goals and desired outcomes.

This competency is important in two ways. First, facilitators must be able to persuade trainees to consider points of view that will lead to desired changes in behavior. Many times a facilitator is asked to sell an organization's culture or policies, or just to gain learners' participation to achieve the desired results of the training. To do this, a facilitator must be able to help trainees understand and accept the organization's realities and practices and, at the same time, be sensitive to their own views. Second,

continued on next page

Assessment 11–4, *continued*
Facilitator Competencies

an effective facilitator needs to know how to form small groups and work well with them to influence their drive to accomplish tasks, work through problems, and fulfill the needs of other group members. When the facilitator is able to draw out the creative energy of groups through brainstorming or other activities, as well as help group members blend their unique knowledge and skills to achieve a common goal, it will lead to greater commitment on behalf of the learners to change their behavior for the better and apply the training content.

9. **Feedback.** Gives and receives constructive, specific, and timely feedback and communicates observations clearly and accurately.

Providing learners with helpful feedback, whether formally through an assessment or informally through conversation, is a vital skill for facilitators. Specific examples that communicate a learner's strengths and weaknesses will help the trainee better comprehend the information and may also lead to increased self-reflection by the learner. Feedback can also serve as the basis for a coaching relationship for individual training and clarify the most important thing for the learner to focus on for his or her growth and development. The facilitator must also be familiar with a variety of tools to gather feedback from training participants to improve the learning experience; the feedback can be helpful for the facilitator's own self-reflection and growth, as well.

10. **Motivation.** Encourages learners to participate and achieve desired results. Generates enthusiasm and commitment from others.

One of the many responsibilities of a training facilitator is to inspire others to achieve the desired outcomes of a training session and to focus on their goals. Although it is generally believed that motivation comes from within, a skilled facilitator can create a vision that motivates and inspires, which will unleash the energy and enthusiasm of the learners. The facilitator can use meaningful learning activities and infuse fun into the training experience; it's his or her responsibility to channel trainees' motivation effectively into a commitment to achieve results.

11. **Organizational skills.** Works in an orderly and logical way to accomplish tasks. Ensures that work is correct and complete. Presents ideas logically and sequentially for learners to understand.

The importance of this competency for facilitators is twofold. One aspect is that the facilitator must have good work habits and pay attention to detail. With any training event, there are a myriad of logistical and other details to take care of to ensure a successful experience. Work must be done thoroughly and accurately. A well-organized training facilitator typically creates well-organized, professional training. Another aspect of this competency is that facilitators must train in a manner that allows learners to absorb new content easily, as well as be able to retrieve it quickly. When information

continued on next page

Assessment 11–4, *continued*
Facilitator Competencies

is presented in a logical, sequential order for greater understanding, there is a higher probability that the learners will use the content. The more organized the facilitator, the better the training event.

12. **Time management**. Plans and prioritizes time effectively. Balances important and urgent tasks and can work on multiple tasks simultaneously.

One of the many things facilitators do is conduct training sessions. They must also be able to budget their time well to tend to other priorities in their work, because they must prepare for the training, keep accurate records, analyze assessment data, design new content or activities, and report to the client organization. The most competent facilitators are able to multitask and stay focused on the goals of the learners and client organization. Good time management is an essential part of the facilitator's ability to stay on top of all there is to do during any given day.

Facilitator Competencies

Instructions: If this instrument is a self-assessment, place a ✓ in the box to the right of each of the 12 facilitator competencies that best describes your skill level. If this form provides feedback to a facilitator, place a ✓ in the box that best fits his or her level of competence in each area.

COMPETENCY	NO EXPERTISE	LITTLE EXPERTISE	SOME EXPERTISE	ADEQUATE EXPERTISE	EXPERT
Understanding adult learners. Uses knowledge of the principles of adult learning to design and deliver training.	☐	☐	☐	☐	☐
Presentation skills. Presents content clearly to achieve the desired outcomes of the training. Encourages learners to generate their own answers through effectively leading group discussions.	☐	☐	☐	☐	☐
Communication skills. Expresses self well, verbally and in writing. Understands nonverbal communication and listens effectively.	☐	☐	☐	☐	☐
Emotional intelligence. Respects learners' viewpoints, knowledge, and experience.	☐	☐	☐	☐	☐

continued on next page

Assessment 11–4, continued
Facilitator Competencies

COMPETENCY	NO EXPERTISE	LITTLE EXPERTISE	SOME EXPERTISE	ADEQUATE EXPERTISE	EXPERT
Recognizes and responds appropriately to others' feelings, attitudes, and concerns.					
Training methods. Varies instructional approaches to address different learning styles and hold learners' interest.	☐	☐	☐	☐	☐
Subject matter expertise. Possesses deep knowledge of training content and applicable experience to draw upon.	☐	☐	☐	☐	☐
Questioning skills. Asks questions in a way that stimulates learners' understanding and curiosity. Encourages critical thinking.	☐	☐	☐	☐	☐
Eliciting behavior change. Influences others effectively, both individually and within groups. Gains support and commitment from others to achieve common goals and desired outcomes.	☐	☐	☐	☐	☐
Feedback. Gives and receives constructive, specific, and timely feedback and communicates observations clearly and accurately.	☐	☐	☐	☐	☐
Motivation. Encourages learners to participate and achieve desired results. Generates enthusiasm and commitment from others.	☐	☐	☐	☐	☐
Organizational skills. Works in an orderly and logical way to accomplish tasks. Ensures work is correct and complete. Presents ideas logically and sequentially for learners to understand.	☐	☐	☐	☐	☐
Time management. Plans and prioritizes time effectively. Balances important and urgent tasks and can work on multiple tasks simultaneously.	☐	☐	☐	☐	☐

Assessment 11–5
Negotiation Skills Follow-Up Assessment

Instructions: This form focuses on the outcomes of the training in which the learner recently participated. Please give your open and honest assessment of the person's current performance. On the line to the left, write a number from 1 to 6 that best corresponds to the scale below to rate the person on some of the more important behaviors for a good negotiator.

Participant Code:

_____

---

1 = HIGHLY INEFFECTIVE   4 = SOMEWHAT EFFECTIVE

2 = INEFFECTIVE   5 = EFFECTIVE

3 = SOMEWHAT INEFFECIVE   6 = HIGHLY EFFECTIVE

The negotiator...

_____ Focuses on the core issues of the negotiation.

_____ Establishes eye contact when he or she addresses negotiation counterparts.

_____ Looks for common areas of interests with the other party.

_____ Listens to a counterpart without judgment or criticism.

_____ Does not interrupt to make his or her points during a negotiation conversation.

_____ Maintains his or her professionalism at all times.

_____ Seeks a win-win solution as much as possible.

_____ Asks questions to get information that could affect the outcome of a negotiation.

_____ Does not react emotionally when he or she disagrees with a counterpart.

_____ Uses negotiation tactics that complement the counterpart's style.

_____ Gets a clear written agreement with action steps and deadlines.

_____ Creates a nonthreatening environment.

Assessment 11–6

Training Evaluation

Your Name: _____ Date: _____

Workshop Title: _____

Facilitator: _____ Location: _____

Please circle the number that best corresponds to your ratings for today's training session.

ITEM		POOR	FAIR	GOOD	EXCELLENT
1.	Quality of the workshop content	1	2	3	4
2.	Applicability of content to my work	1	2	3	4
3.	Quality of training materials/handouts	1	2	3	4
4.	Quality of audio-visual materials	1	2	3	4
5.	Facilitator's presentation skills	1	2	3	4
6.	Facilitator's knowledge of subject	1	2	3	4
7.	Amount of participant interaction	1	2	3	4
8.	Time allotted for activities	1	2	3	4
9.	Facility/location	1	2	3	4
10.	Overall workshop rating	1	2	3	4

Would you recommend this session to a colleague? Why or why not? _____

_____

_____

_____

_____

How will you begin to apply the training content after today's session? _____

_____

_____

_____

_____

Assessment 11–7
Nonverbal Communication Self-Assessment

Instructions: Use this assessment to determine how and where you can improve when you give and receive nonverbal feedback. Place a ✓ in one of the boxes to the right of each item. Please complete the assessment based on how you behave right now and give honest responses; no one will see the results unless you choose to share them.

NONVERBAL COMMUNICATION BEHAVIORS	TO A GREAT EXTENT	FOR THE MOST PART	TO SOME EXTENT	NOT AT ALL
When I give nonverbal feedback, I...				
1. Adapt my nonverbal response to the situation.	☐	☐	☐	☐
2. Match my verbal communication.	☐	☐	☐	☐
3. Vary my voice pitch and volume.	☐	☐	☐	☐
4. Use appropriate gestures to show interest.	☐	☐	☐	☐
5. Keep good eye contact when in conversation.	☐	☐	☐	☐
6. Maintain a professional posture.	☐	☐	☐	☐
7. Vary my facial expressions as appropriate.	☐	☐	☐	☐
When I receive nonverbal feedback, I...				
8. Check that it matches the verbal message.	☐	☐	☐	☐
9. Pick up on nonverbal cues quickly.	☐	☐	☐	☐
10. Interpret others' messages correctly.	☐	☐	☐	☐
11. Respond with appropriate feedback.	☐	☐	☐	☐
12. Consider cultural differences in nonverbal communication signals.	☐	☐	☐	☐
13. Watch the giver's facial expressions.	☐	☐	☐	☐
14. Notice subtle gestures and movement.	☐	☐	☐	☐

continued on next page

Assessment 11–7, continued

Nonverbal Communication Self-Assessment

Analysis: The results of this assessment can help direct your focus for areas of improvement as a giver or receiver of nonverbal feedback. You may find that you score higher as a giver than as a receiver, or that you score higher on particular items in either category.

As a giver of nonverbal feedback, if you rated yourself in the "To Some Extent" or "Not At All" areas for items 1, 2, 5, or 6, this means that you should pay particular attention to others' moods, emotions, and circumstances in the interaction and adapt accordingly. If you scored low on items 3, 4, or 7, you may need to try to keep the receiver's interest through your nonverbal communication.

As a receiver of nonverbal feedback, ratings in the "To Some Extent" or "Not At All" areas for items 8–14 indicate a need to be more sensitive to others' nonverbal messages and to improve your focus on the meaning of the giver. You may also need to pay attention to your own nonverbal responses and find ways to minimize any negative or defensive behaviors.

Training Instrument 11–1

Negotiation Conversation Preparation Sheet
(for Structured Experience 12–5: Preparation Practice)

Preparing to Negotiate

What is the desired outcome of the negotiation?

What is your BATNA (Best Alternative to a Negotiated Agreement)? How can you improve your BATNA?

What are your primary interests in the negotiation?
"Must Haves"   **"Nice to Haves"**

What are the other side's primary interests in the negotiation?
"Must Haves"   **"Nice to Haves"**

What are the possible trade-offs you'd be willing to make?

Who will be involved in the negotiation?

continued on next page

Training Instrument 11–1, continued
Negotiation Conversation Preparation Sheet
(for Structured Experience 12–5: Preparation Practice)

What are the behavioral styles of the people involved? **Name**	**Style**
What are some strategies you will use to counterbalance these styles?	
Who on each side has the authority to make a deal?	
What criteria and standards will be used in the negotiation?	
How will both sides communicate during the negotiation?	
What else do you know about the other side's organization or industry?	
How will you build rapport and trust with the other side?	
How will you gain commitment from the other side?	

Adapted from: Watkins, Michael. *Negotiation*. Boston: Harvard Business School Press, 2003.

Training Instrument 11–2

Brainstorming Checklist
(for Structured Experience 12–6: Brainstorming Best Practices)

Instructions: This checklist is designed to help you provide feedback to the participants in the small-group brainstorming exercise. Put a ✓ in one of the boxes to the right of each statement, depending on whether you observed the behavior as described. There is also a space for comments to share with the other participants.

DID THE GROUP:	YES	NO	NOT SURE
1. Welcome all ideas without judgment?	☐	☐	☐
2. Accurately capture all ideas in writing?	☐	☐	☐
3. Clarify any ideas that were unclear?	☐	☐	☐
4. Pay attention and avoid interruptions?	☐	☐	☐
5. Receive ideas from each participant?	☐	☐	☐
6. Narrow the list of options for consideration?	☐	☐	☐
7. Sit facing each other to see all participants?	☐	☐	☐
8. Prioritize options and decide next steps?	☐	☐	☐
9. Appear to have fun and be relaxed?	☐	☐	☐
10. Quickly and easily choose a spokesperson?	☐	☐	☐

COMMENTS FOR THE GROUP:

_____

_____

_____

_____

_____

_____

Training Instrument 11–3

Negotiation Success Plan
(for Structured Experience 12–12: What a Success!)

My Plan for a Successful Negotiation

My organization's goal for this negotiation is:
My counterpart's goal for this negotiation is:
I will know the negotiation is successful by measuring:
I will use the following strategy to learn the other side's BATNA (Best Alternative to a Negotiated Agreement):
I will use the following tactics to build the relationship with my counterpart:
I will use the following strategies to investigate interests with my counterpart:
I will use the following strategy to work with the other side to set negotiation criteria and fair standards:
I will help create an open, inviting atmosphere in negotiation conversations by:
I will ensure a specific action plan for the negotiation is in place through:

Adapted from: Watkins, Michael. *Negotiation.* Boston: Harvard Business School Press, 2003.

Training Instrument 11–4
Facilitation Preparation Checklist

This instrument is designed to help you as the facilitator prepare for a training session by ensuring that you have all of the materials and equipment necessary to conduct a workshop. All pretraining activities and needed materials and tools are listed to help you prepare for a successful session. Specific materials will vary based on the content modules you will use for the training.

Pretraining Activities

☐ Reviewed learning needs-assessment data to ensure effective selection of content.

☐ Read and reviewed applicable content modules and structured experiences.

☐ Read and reviewed applicable assessments and participant handouts.

☐ Reviewed all PowerPoint slides thoroughly.

☐ Prepared additional anecdotes and examples.

☐ Practiced workshop flow and exercises.

Workshop Materials and Tools

☐ Content module and structured experience instructions

☐ Content module PowerPoint slide decks

☐ LCD projector with screen

☐ Computer and cables

☐ Power strip and extension cord

☐ Participant handouts, assessments, and instruments

☐ Attendance and registration sheet or participant sign-in sheet

☐ Participant name tags and table tent cards (if applicable)

☐ Facilitator and training evaluations

☐ Writing instruments (pens, pencils, and markers)

☐ Extra paper (if participants need it)

☐ Flipchart with easel and markers (or whiteboard in training room)

☐ Masking tape to post chart paper (if paper is not self-adhesive)

continued on next page

Training Instrument 11–4, continued
Facilitation Preparation Checklist

☐ Facilitator table or podium (to hold workshop materials)

☐ Watch or other timepiece for structured experiences and workshop flow

☐ Supplemental materials for structured experiences (such as prizes for activities)

☐ Toys or candy for participants at tables (optional)

☐ Facilitator's business cards (if external to the organization) to give to participants

◆

Structured Experiences

What's in This Chapter?

- ◆ Explanation of structured experiences

- ◆ Step-by-step instructions for using structured experiences

- ◆ Structured Experiences 12–1 through 12–12

This chapter contains 12 structured experiences to assist in the learning process. A structured experience is a step-by-step design that applies adult learning principles. Each experience includes:

- ◆ **Goals.** The learning outcomes that the experience is designed to achieve.

- ◆ **Materials.** A listing of all materials required to facilitate the experience.

- ◆ **Time.** Anticipated time allowances for each step of the experience. These can vary based on the facilitator and the participants.

- ◆ **Instructions.** Step-by-step instructions to facilitate the experience.

- ◆ **Debriefing.** Suggested debriefing topics and questions. These should be modified to meet the needs of the participants.

The Structured Experiences

Each of the following designs is self-contained. Although some of the experiences are designed specifically for learning outcomes associated with the module they support, others can be used in a variety of modules that the trainer either currently uses or is developing.

- ◆ **Structured Experience 12–1: Negotiation Partners.** In this structured experience a pair of participants conducts a simple negotiation with each other. They share what they learned during the activity with the group as a way to gauge their negotiation skills. It is part of Content Module 10–2: Types of Negotiations.

- ◆ **Structured Experience 12–2: Negotiation Scenarios.** This exercise asks participants to determine various situations in which they negotiate, whether or not they are aware of using negotiation skills, to emphasize how often we negotiate. It is used in Content Module 10–2: Types of Negotiations.

- ◆ **Structured Experience 12–3: BATNA Basics.** In this exercise, participants analyze their own and a negotiation counterpart's wants and needs, as well as identify a strong versus weak BATNA (*Best Alternative To a Negotiated Agreement*). It is part of Content Module 10–4: Core Principles of Negotiation.

- ◆ **Structured Experience 12–4: Nonverbal Negotiation.** In this fun and engaging exercise, participants work in small groups to demonstrate types of nonverbal communication to illustrate how nonverbal feedback can influence a negotiation conversation. It supports Content Module 10–5: Steps to Negotiation.

- ◆ **Structured Experience 12–5: Preparation Practice.** This structured experience asks participants to complete a preparation sheet for a negotiation conversation as a planning method. It is used Content Module 10–5: Steps to Negotiation.

- ◆ **Structured Experience 12–6: Brainstorming Best Practices.** In this energizing exercise, participants practice brainstorming strategies as a way to investigate common interests with a negotiation counterpart. It is part of Content Module 10–6: Investigating Interests.

- ◆ **Structured Experience 12–7: Out of the Question.** Participants work together in this interactive exercise to create effective questions to use before and during a negotiation conversation to extract information from a negotiation counterpart. It supports Content Module 10–7: Building Trust and Relationships.

- **Structured Experience 12–8: A Different Point of View.** This exercise shows participants how consideration of different points of view in various aspects of negotiation can lead to success. It is part of Content Module 10–7: Building Trust and Relationships.

- **Structured Experience 12–9: Tactics Testing.** Participants have fun in this entertaining exercise when they identify common tactics negotiators use. It is a powerful way to illustrate the array of approaches used in a negotiation conversation. It supports Content Module 10–8: Negotiation Tactics.

- **Structured Experience 12–10: Beyond the Barriers.** In this role-play exercise, participants take on various personas to have negotiation conversations with each other to overcome obstacles. Volunteers may also hone their skills in front of the group. It supports Content Module 10–9: Barriers to Negotiation.

- **Structured Experience 12–11: Examining Ethics.** This exercise lets participants examine a negotiation case study and identify particular ethical approaches used in bargaining. It is part of Content Module 10–10: Ethics in Negotiation.

- **Structured Experience 12–12: What a Success!** In this exercise, participants use a strategic planning tool to set their negotiations up for success and evaluate their effectiveness. It is used in Content Module 10–11: Negotiation Success Factors.

The Handouts

Four of the structured experiences in this chapter include handouts (in the online materials) as part of the content for the activities. Feel free to adapt these as needed.

- **Handout 12–1: Nonverbal Communication Chart**. Part of Structured Experience 12–4: Nonverbal Negotiation, this handout serves as a reference for participants to help them associate some nonverbal communication with certain emotions.

- **Handout 12–2: Common Negotiation Tactics**. Used in Structured Experience 12–9: Tactics Testing, this handout is used in a small-group activity to define some of the more common tactics used in negotiation conversations.

◆ **Handout 12–3: Barrier Role-Play Scenarios**. Distributed during Structured Experience 12–10: Beyond the Barriers, this handout provides scenarios for participants to review and act out as part of a role-play activity.

◆ **Handout 12–4: Ethics Case Study**. Part of Structured Experience 12–11: Examining Ethics, this handout includes a case study of an ethical issue for a particular negotiation that participants can analyze and discuss in small groups.

Structured Experience 12–1: Negotiation Partners

GOALS

The goals of this experience are to

- ◆ Allow participants to interact and learn about each other.

- ◆ Gauge their negotiation skills in a learning environment.

MATERIALS

None

TIME

- ◆ 5 minutes for introduction and setup of the exercise

- ◆ 15 minutes for discussion in pairs

- ◆ 10 minutes for debriefing

INSTRUCTIONS

1. Divide participants into pairs. If the number of participants is odd, form one group of three.

2. Tell participants to engage in a 10-minute conversation in which each partner negotiates for an item in the other's possession (for example, a notebook, a pen, or a jacket) for five minutes. During each person's chance to negotiate, the owner of the item may ask clarifying questions and provide short responses, but otherwise should not talk. The owner should concentrate as much as possible on what the negotiator says and should try to notice the tactics of persuasion the negotiator uses. Time the exercise so participants know when to switch roles. In a group of three, the participants should divide the time accordingly so each has a chance to negotiate.

3. At the end of the 10-minute conversation time, allow the partners five minutes to share what each remembers about the persuasion tactics used from the conversations. Provide a time update when two minutes remain.

DEBRIEFING

Ask for a handful of volunteer participants to share some of the more interesting tactics of persuasion they encountered during the activity and what they noticed about their partner's negotiation style. Lead a discussion of how the group performed as negotiators, as well as what it was like to negotiate with little time to prepare. (10 minutes)

Structured Experience 12–2: Negotiation Scenarios

GOALS

The goals of this experience are to

◆ Reinforce the idea that we negotiate on a regular basis.

◆ Help participants recognize when they are in a negotiation.

◆ Get participants in touch with their negotiation style.

MATERIALS

The materials needed for this structured experience are

◆ Writing instruments

◆ Blank paper to take notes

◆ A flipchart or whiteboard with markers to record participants' scenarios

TIME

◆ 5 minutes for introduction and setup

◆ 15 minutes to brainstorm and share negotiation situations

◆ 10 minutes for debriefing

INSTRUCTIONS

1. Ask participants to take out a sheet of paper and a pen or pencil.

2. Explain that for the next five minutes their task is to think of and write down as many situations as they can in which they negotiated for something in the last week. Provide them with some examples, such as getting their children to eat dinner, setting an appointment date and time, deciding on a movie to see with their families, or getting an estimate for car repairs. (5 minutes)

3. When ready to start the timed portion, ask participants not to say anything for this portion of the exercise.

4. Once the time in silence has passed, ask the participants to walk around the room and compare the negotiation situations they noted with those that fellow participants wrote down to see whether any common characteristics exist. (5 minutes)

5. Ask the participants to return to their seats and share some of their negotiation scenarios with the large group. Chart these on a flipchart or whiteboard for everyone to see. Request that people raise their hands if the situation is one they also noted. (5 minutes)

DEBRIEFING

Lead a discussion in which you ask the group the questions below. The theme for the debriefing is to point out that we negotiate on a regular basis, yet we may not always recognize when we do it. Similarly, it's important to identify situations in which someone negotiates with us in order to have a successful outcome. (10 minutes)

1. How many of you had situations in common with others in the group?

2. For those who did not, were you surprised by this? Why or why not?

3. What are the implications of this exercise about how and when we negotiate?

4. What did you observe about the items you noted during the silent portion of the exercise?

5. When you think about your negotiation situations, how would you assess your typical approach to a negotiation conversation?

Structured Experience 12–3: BATNA Basics

GOALS

The goals of this experience are to

- ◆ Enable participants to identify wants versus needs correctly.

- ◆ Teach participants the advantages of having a strong BATNA (*Best Al-*
  ternative To a Negotiated Agreement).

- ◆ Reinforce the importance of knowing the other side's needs.

MATERIALS

The materials needed for this structured experience are

- ◆ Writing instruments

- ◆ Blank paper for taking notes

TIME

- ◆ 5 minutes for introduction and setup

- ◆ 5 minutes to record wants and needs for negotiation scenarios

- ◆ 5 minutes to record the BATNA for each side in a negotiation

- ◆ 10 minutes to share wants, needs, and BATNAs with a partner

- ◆ 10 minutes to rewrite and share BATNAs

- ◆ 10 minutes for debriefing

INSTRUCTIONS

1. Ask participants to take out a sheet of paper and a pen or pencil.

2. Explain that they will learn to distinguish between a want and a need,
   using either a current or past work-related negotiation situation. Tell
   them to take five minutes to think of a negotiation situation they
   would like to work with and then write down their wants and needs
   for the negotiation to be successful. When finished with their situation, they should then write down what the other side's wants and
   needs may be.

3. Once the five-minute period has passed, ask the participants to go through the same process to record their situation and what they think the other side's BATNA could be for the same negotiation situation used in step 2. They should pay particular attention to what their alternatives will be if an agreement cannot be reached, any better arrangements they could make with other parties not currently involved in the negotiation, and any terms of a possible agreement they could change if necessary.

4. When finished, divide the group into pairs. If the number of participants is uneven, form one group of three.

5. Allow approximately 10 minutes for the pairs to share the wants, needs, and BATNAs for their negotiation scenarios with each other and seek feedback as if their partner is their negotiation counterpart. As the "other side," the participants should tell their partner if the wants, needs, and BATNA are accurate or if changes need to be made.

6. When time is up, allow five minutes for the participants to rewrite their BATNA and their "counterpart's" BATNA and another five minutes for everyone to share the new BATNAs with their partner.

7. Begin the debriefing when participants have finished.

DEBRIEFING

Lead the debriefing into a discussion of the possible advantages of a strong BATNA, as well as how important it is to have a good idea of your negotiation counterpart's BATNA and needs. Ask participants to share any troubles they may have had when they identified wants and needs, as well as what insights they have gained about negotiation after this exercise. (10 minutes)

Structured Experience 12–4: Nonverbal Negotiation

GOALS

The goals of this structured experience are to

- ◆ Illustrate the importance of nonverbal communication in negotiation conversations.

- ◆ Explore nonverbal behaviors that occur during negotiation.

- ◆ Build relationships among participants.

MATERIALS

The materials needed for this structured experience are

- ◆ Writing instruments

- ◆ Blank paper to take notes

- ◆ Copies of Handout 12–1: Nonverbal Communication Chart for all participants

- ◆ A flipchart or whiteboard with markers to record participants' nonverbal feedback

TIME

- ◆ 5 minutes to form groups and for setup

- ◆ 15 minutes for small-group discussions

- ◆ 10 minutes for groups to share nonverbal feedback

- ◆ 15 minutes for debriefing

INSTRUCTIONS

1. Divide participants into groups, each with four or five people. Have them move their chairs so they face each other in a circle, if possible. They will need to have some freedom of movement away from tables for this exercise.

2. In their groups, tell the participants they will have five minutes to brainstorm as many nonverbal communication behaviors as possible (for example, crossing one's arms, rolling one's eyes, and pacing).

3. When time is up, allow 10 minutes for the groups to assign emotions to each nonverbal communication they listed (for example, pacing can indicate nervousness).

4. After 10 minutes, ask the group to choose four or five of the nonverbal behaviors (one for each group member) to act out for the large group. They should select behaviors that could have more than one emotional meaning.

5. When ready, ask the first group to come up to the front of room. When you say "go," each group member should display his or her selected nonverbal behavior. As the group members act out their behaviors, the others in the room should shout out the emotions they see displayed by the nonverbal communication in front of them. Chart the emotions the large group shares. When the first group is done, ask the next group to act out their nonverbal behaviors and the large group to shout out the emotions they see while you chart them. Continue this process until each small group has had a turn. This portion of the activity should take approximately 10 minutes.

6. After each group has had a turn and the emotions are charted, give everyone a copy of Handout 12–1: Nonverbal Communication Chart, and briefly review it before you start the debriefing discussion.

DEBRIEFING

While in their small groups, debrief the participants to compare the list of emotions they helped create in the large-group portion of the exercise with those listed on Handout 12–1. Ask them to also compare the nonverbal behaviors on the handout with the ones they brainstormed in their small groups. Then, use the following questions to help lead the debriefing. When discussion is finished, ask the participants to return to their original seats. (15 minutes)

1. How many nonverbal behaviors and emotions do you see on the handout that are similar to those you brainstormed in your small groups and acted out in front of the large group? How do you explain any matches?

2. Why is it important that we pay attention to nonverbal communication when we negotiate?

3. What happens when we don't pay attention to nonverbal communication in conversations?

4. What did you notice during this exercise about your own nonverbal behavior?

5. What strategies can you use to adapt your behavior to nonverbal feedback you receive during negotiations?

Structured Experience 12–5: Preparation Practice

GOALS

The goals of this experience are to

◆ Allow participants to prepare for a negotiation conversation.

◆ Demonstrate the effectiveness of a tool to prepare for negotiation.

◆ Engage participants to think about aspects of negotiation they may not pay attention to in a typical situation.

MATERIALS

The materials needed for this structured experience are

◆ Writing instruments

◆ Copies of Training Instrument 11–1: Negotiation Conversation Preparation Sheet for all participants

TIME

◆ 5 minutes for setup

◆ 10 minutes for participants to complete preparation

◆ 10 minutes to share preparation sheet with partner

◆ 5 minutes for debriefing

INSTRUCTIONS

1. Give each participant a copy of Training Instrument 11–1: Negotiation Conversation Preparation Sheet and review the items on the tool.

2. Ask the participants to take out a pen or pencil and to think about either an upcoming work-related negotiation conversation they need to have or one that they are working on as part of a team. If they do not have an upcoming negotiation, ask them to use a recent situation, regardless of the negotiation's actual outcome.

3. Explain that for the next 10 minutes, the participants need to complete the preparation sheet and fill in as much information as they

know (or can at least approximate) for the negotiation counterpart in their negotiation situation.

4. When time is up, ask the participants to find a partner. If the number of participants is uneven, one group of three will work.

5. Allow 10 minutes for the participants to share their preparation sheets with their partners (5 minutes per person) to explain the negotiation situation they are working on and to gauge the effectiveness of their plans, as if their partner were on their negotiation team. Encourage the partner who listens to think about what the other partner says as if the listener were a team member of the speaker. The listener should provide feedback to the speaker, assuming this team member role.

6. After 10 minutes, ask the participants to return to their original seats and begin the debriefing discussion.

DEBRIEFING

Debrief participants on the effectiveness of a tool like the preparation sheet to help them get ready for a negotiation conversation. Ask them their reactions to the feedback they received from their partner, as well as how helpful that portion of the exercise was for them. You may also ask for a handful of volunteers to share the information they wrote on the preparation sheet, providing background information on the situation, to survey the large group on the effectiveness of the individuals' plans. (5 minutes)

Structured Experience 12–6: Brainstorming Best Practices

GOALS

The goals of this experience are to

- Demonstrate the effectiveness of brainstorming as a way to investigate common interests during negotiations.

- Practice brainstorming guidelines.

- Have fun.

MATERIALS

The materials needed for this structured experience are

- Writing instruments

- Copies of Training Instrument 11-2: Brainstorming Checklist for five to six participants (one for each small group)

- Loose sheets of flipchart paper for small groups (one per group)

- Markers for participants to use in small groups (one per group)

TIME

- 10 minutes for setup and to choose negotiation scenarios

- 20–30 minutes for participants to brainstorm interests in small groups (exact timing is dependent upon group size) and receive feedback

- 5 minutes for debriefing

INSTRUCTIONS

1. Divide participants into groups, each with five to six people. Ask them to gather at a spot around the perimeter of the room and give one marker and one sheet of flipchart paper to each group. The group should affix the chart paper to the wall to use as a writing surface.

2. Ask for each small group to designate an observer who will record some information while the others brainstorm. Provide each observer with a copy of Training Instrument 11–2: Brainstorming Checklist.

3. Ask the participants, in their small groups, to think of a simple negotiation situation around which they would like to brainstorm interests (for example, buying a car, hiring a remodeling contractor, or deciding on a college for their child to attend).

4. Next, they need to divide themselves (as equally as possible) to represent each side in the negotiation (two to three people per side, excluding the observer).

5. Once each group has thought of a scenario and a side, tell them that for the next 15–20 minutes they should engage in a brainstorming session to discover common interests that are important to their side. Someone in the group should write these interests on the flipchart paper, and it is the job of the observer to complete the checklist as the group brainstorms.

6. When time is up (typically, the smaller the overall group size, the less time is needed for brainstorming), ask the observers to share their feedback from the checklist with their respective small groups. Allow 5–10 minutes for this.

7. Once they have received all observer feedback, ask the participants to return to their original seats and start the debriefing discussion.

DEBRIEFING (5 MINUTES)

1. What observations do they have about their group's brainstorming behavior during the exercise?

2. How many interests did they have in common for each side in their small groups? Was this surprising? Why or why not?

3. What is some of the feedback they received from the observer in their small groups? What is the impact of this feedback?

4. What will they do differently, if anything, when they engage in brainstorming activities in the future?

5. How will they personally use brainstorming in negotiations?

Structured Experience 12–7: Out of the Question

GOALS

The goals of this experience are to

- Demonstrate how important it is to ask good questions of a negotiation counterpart to extract useful data.

- Practice writing effective questions.

- Build relationships among participants.

MATERIALS

The materials needed for this structured experience are

- Writing instruments

- Blank paper to take notes

- A flipchart or whiteboard with markers to record participants' questions

TIME

- 5 minutes for setup

- 10 minutes for large-group question brainstorming

- 15 minutes for partner work

- 10 minutes for debriefing

INSTRUCTIONS

1. Tell the participants that, for about 10 minutes, the large group will brainstorm questions they could ask a negotiation counterpart to acquire information that could be helpful in a negotiation. You may either suggest a negotiation scenario for the group to work with, such as negotiating a price to purchase items from a vendor that your company will turn around and sell, or ask the group to suggest a scenario. Ideally, the negotiation situation is one that is applicable to the group.

2. Once a scenario is decided, help the group brainstorm questions they could ask a negotiation counterpart (someone who, presumably, would be a logical choice for the scenario) in an attempt to gain information about the counterpart's needs, interests, and behavioral style, as well as to verify information, build rapport, or check understanding. Write the group's questions on a flipchart or whiteboard. Allow approximately 10 minutes for this portion of the activity.

3. After this brainstorming period, ask the participants to find a partner with whom to work (one group of three will work if the number of learners is uneven).

4. Allow 5 minutes for the participants to brainstorm questions they could ask their partner, as if their partner were their negotiation counterpart, following the same brainstorming process as was done in the large group. Ask the participants to work with a current negotiation situation or one that happened in the past to generate their questions.

5. When time is up, tell the participants that they will each have five minutes to interview each other, using the questions they created. The other person should assume the role of the negotiation counterpart (they should be provided with any necessary background about the scenario their partner selected). After the first five minutes, stop the interview and ask the participants to switch roles.

6. After both partners have completed their interviews, ask the participants to return to their seats and begin the debriefing discussion.

DEBRIEFING (10 MINUTES)

1. What is your reaction to this exercise? How does brainstorming a list of questions prior to your negotiation conversation help you be more effective?

2. What effect did your questions have on the interview? Did you get some good information from your "counterpart?"

3. What did you notice about your own behavior as the person who was interviewed? Did you share more as a result of the questions?

4. What did you notice about your behavior as the interviewer? Did you listen carefully to the responses from your partner?

5. How will you use this questioning technique specifically in your work?

Structured Experience 12–8: A Different Point of View

GOALS

The goals of this experience are to

- Illustrate how consideration of all parties' points of view in a negotiation leads to successful outcomes.

- Enable participants to analyze their own point of view for a negotiation.

- Share strategies for how to uncover others' points of view.

MATERIALS

Materials needed for this structured experience are

- Writing instruments

- Blank paper to take notes

- A flipchart or whiteboard with markers to record participants' point of view data

TIME

- 10 minutes for setup

- 10 minutes for individual work to think about point of view

- 15 minutes to share point of view situations and group feedback

- 10 minutes for debriefing

INSTRUCTIONS

1. Ask participants to take out some paper and a pen or pencil.

2. Tell each participant that, for the next 10 minutes, he or she should think about and write down his or her own point of view and a negotiation counterpart's point of view for a past or future negotiation situation. This can be either a work-related or family-related situation that they would be willing to share with the group. Ask the participants to address the following items for both sides:

Goal of the negotiation   *Personal biases*

Facts of the situation   *Position on issue*

Sources of needed information   *Behavioral styles*

Needs and wants   *Environment*

Note: It may be helpful for the facilitator to walk through an example for the participants, so have a simple negotiation situation prepared ahead of time, such as how to decide on a family vacation destination or discuss with a spouse where to retire.

3. After the 10-minute period, ask for a volunteer to share his or her example with the large group, preferably at the front of the room. As the volunteer speaks, write down on a flipchart or whiteboard the key point of view information he or she provides. When finished, ask the group what feedback they have for the volunteer. Does the volunteer's assessment of point of view seem comprehensive? Is there anything else the group would want to consider in this negotiation situation? Repeat this process with two or three other volunteers as time allows, taking approximately 15 minutes for this portion of the activity.

4. When ready, move on to the debriefing.

DEBRIEFING

Debrief around the idea that often we jump to conclusions when we hear information or interact with someone, and it is important to stop and think about others' points of view in a negotiation situation, as well as our own. Otherwise, it is possible to miss critical information or ignore important data, especially if we are biased toward a particular person or course of action. (10 minutes)

1. Ask participants to share any examples of a time when they may have jumped to conclusions about a negotiation counterpart or when someone they negotiated with made assumptions about them. What was the result?

2. Lead the debriefing into a discussion of what can be done in negotiation situations to avoid incorrect assumptions and how this could affect a successful outcome.

Structured Experience 12–9: Tactics Testing

GOALS

The goals of this experience are to

* Demonstrate the power of common negotiation tactics.

* Explore how to use tactics strategically.

* Have fun.

MATERIALS

* Writing instruments

* Candy or other small prizes (optional)

* Copies of Handout 12–2: Common Negotiation Tactics for all participants

* A flipchart or whiteboard with markers to record participants' scores

TIME

* 5 minutes for setup

* 10 minutes for partner work on page 1 of handout

* 10 minutes for comparison of tactics definitions

* 10 minutes to read definitions and scoring

* 5 minutes for debriefing

INSTRUCTIONS

1. Give each participant a copy of page 1 of Handout 12–2: Common Negotiation Tactics. Be sure to provide only the first page, as the second page will be used later in the exercise.

2. Briefly review the items on page 1. Explain that these tactics are some of the many that can be used in negotiation situations, and that they may, in fact, already use some of them or at least have been on the receiving end of many.

3. Ask the participants to find a partner (one group of three works well if the number of learners is uneven).

4. Explain that, for the next 10 minutes, their task with their partner is to create definitions for each of the tactics listed on page 1 of the handout. The definitions do not need to be lengthy; just a sentence or two is fine.

5. When time is up, allow 10 minutes for the pairs to move around the room and compare their definitions with the other participants' definitions. Check to see if they appear to be on track, and ask the participants' definitions to sit down again with their partners.

6. Next, explain that there will now be a competition to see who got the definitions correct. Use page 2 of Handout 12–2, and ask each pair to read each actual definition aloud. After each definition, check to see which pairs got it correct (exact wording is unnecessary) and record a point on a flipchart or whiteboard for those who got it right. Repeat this process for the remaining definitions, taking approximately 10 minutes for this portion of the activity.

   Note: You may also want to provide example situations to share with the group to illustrate each tactic further (or ask the participants to share examples of each).

7. Tally the scores, and provide prizes (optional) to the winning pair(s). A tie may occur, and that is acceptable.

8. After the game is complete, give each participant a copy of page 2 of Handout 12–2 for reference and begin the debriefing discussion.

DEBRIEFING

Discuss what the participants learned about negotiation tactics from this exercise and which tactics, if any, they have encountered during negotiations or they have used. (5 minutes)

1. Were any of the tactics surprising to them? Why or why not?

2. Are there any they will now try? Which ones and why?

Structured Experience 12–10: Beyond the Barriers

GOALS

The goals for this experience are to

- ◆ Provide participants with an opportunity to practice their negotiation skills.

- ◆ Illustrate that it is possible to overcome barriers to negotiations.

- ◆ Have fun.

MATERIALS

- ◆ Writing instruments

- ◆ Blank paper to take notes

- ◆ Copies of Handout 12–3: Barrier Role-Play Scenarios for all participants

TIME

- ◆ 5 minutes for setup and to form groups

- ◆ 25 minutes for small-group feedback conversations

- ◆ 10 minutes for volunteers to practice in front of large group (optional)

- ◆ 5 minutes for debriefing

INSTRUCTIONS

1. Divide participants into groups, each with three people. If necessary to have three per group, the facilitator may need to join a group and participate in the exercise.

2. Hand out copies of Handout 12–3: Barrier Role-Play Scenarios to all participants.

3. Ask participants to review Handout 12–3 with you and explain that there are three different scenarios. Walk them through the scenarios in the handout and format for the exercise. In their groups, they will have three rounds to switch off and play different roles, working

through each scenario, one at a time, to practice how to overcome the different barriers encountered in negotiations. One person in their group will be an observer who will provide feedback after each round.

4. Give them a moment to decide who will play each role to start for Scenario A. The person who observes should take some notes on how the participants worked through the barriers and be prepared to provide feedback to the players after each round of the exercise.

5. Allow the participants about two minutes to review the scenario, and decide which roles they will play and which approach they will take for the first round. When ready, begin the exercise by asking the first two characters for Scenario A to start the negotiation conversation. Emphasize that the players should remember to use the tips they learned to overcome negotiation barriers to carry out the role-play conversation.

6. Time the exercise. Give the participants approximately four minutes to have their first feedback conversations. When time is up, ask the observers to share their observations with the players for two to three minutes. Let the participants know they have an additional two minutes to share ideas with their groups, such as how they think they did during the conversation and what it felt like.

7. Ask the groups to move on to Scenario B and rotate characters/observers so there is a new observer for the second round. Repeat the process in step 5 above with Scenario B. Follow the procedure in step 6, and move on to a third round with Scenario C so each participant has been an observer.

8. When ready, ask participants to go back to their original seats.

LARGE-GROUP PRACTICE (OPTIONAL)

1. Ask for two volunteers to do the role-play again for the large group (a pair for each of the three scenarios, which builds on what they learned from their small-group experience). Explain that the first round will now be re-created and you need two people to role-play the first negotiation conversation again (Scenario A), but only for two to three minutes this time. The volunteers should go to the front of the room and begin the role play.

2. When the period of two to three minutes has passed, ask the audience to share what they observed about the negotiation conversation and thank the volunteers for their willingness to participate in front of the group.

3. When ready, ask for two new volunteers to re-create the negotiation conversation in round two (Scenario B) and follow the procedures in step two above. Do the same for the round three negotiation conversation (Scenario C) with two new volunteers.

Note: The above portion of this structured experience may not be suitable for all groups. The facilitator will need to gauge the personalities in the group and decide whether the large-group practice would be beneficial and enjoyable for the participants.

DEBRIEFING

Ask for a handful of volunteer participants to share their reactions to the exercise. Lead the debriefing into a discussion of how the participants performed as negotiators and the role that barriers played in the activity, how they used the tips to overcome barriers in negotiations during the experience, and whether they found the information they learned to be helpful. (5 minutes)

Structured Experience 12–11: Examining Ethics

GOALS

The goals for this experience are to

- ♦ Enable participants to gauge their ability to analyze ethical issues.

- ♦ Demonstrate the effectiveness of considering ethics in negotiations.

- ♦ Build relationships among participants.

MATERIALS

Materials needed for this structured experience are

- ♦ Writing instruments

- ♦ Copies of Handout 12–4: Ethics Case Study for all participants

- ♦ A flipchart or whiteboard to record participants' case study questions

TIME

- ♦ 10 minutes for setup and to form small groups

- ♦ 10 minutes to interview the facilitator

- ♦ 20 minutes for case study analysis

- ♦ 10 minutes to share case study decision

- ♦ 10 minutes for debriefing

INSTRUCTIONS

1. Divide participants into groups, each with four or five people.

2. Give copies of Handout 12–4: Ethics Case Study to all participants.

3. Review the case study with the participants and provide a summary of the negotiation situation in the case. Allow approximately three to five minutes for the participants to read the case study.

4. Next, take 10 minutes for the participants to brainstorm questions about the case and the individuals involved in the scenario. Write these questions on flipchart paper or a whiteboard.

5. After 10 minutes, tell the group that they now have an opportunity to ask you the questions they just brainstormed, as you take on the role of one of the parties in the negotiation (you can choose which character in the scenario to portray before the session). Allow 10 minutes for the interview.

6. When time is up, ask the participants to take approximately 20 minutes to discuss the case study in their small groups. They should decide their ethical stance about the situation in the case and create a supporting argument to explain to the large group why they take this position. Participants should also consider the various points of view in the case and note what these may be, as this will also be information they will share.

7. After 20 minutes (time will vary based on size of large group), allow each small group to share the following with the large group: their ethical decision, their reasons for this decision, and their considerations regarding the points of view of the parties involved in the negotiation case. Others may ask clarifying questions during the small-group presentations as necessary, within the time constraint.

8. Ask the groups to rotate roles so there is a new speaker, listener, and observer. Repeat the process in step 5 above. Follow the procedure in step 6 and move on to a third round so each participant has played each role.

9. When ready, ask participants to go back to their original seats and begin the debriefing.

DEBRIEFING

Debrief the exercise around the concept of how important it is to consider ethics in negotiations, as well as the impact it can have if ethical issues are ignored. (10 minutes)

1. How did the small groups decide which decision to make and which approach to take regarding the case? Was it easy for them to come to a conclusion? Why or why not?

2. Have they been in a negotiation situation where there was some questionable behavior? If so, what was the outcome?

3. How will they now watch for possible ethical issues in future negotiations?

Structured Experience 12–12: What a Success!

GOALS

The goals for this experience are to

- ◆ Teach participants to use a tool to develop a negotiation success plan.

- ◆ Illustrate the importance of planning next steps for effective negotiations.

- ◆ Share plans with others for greater commitment and accountability.

MATERIALS

Materials needed for this structured experience are

- ◆ Writing instruments

- ◆ Copies of Training Instrument 11–3: Negotiation Success Plan for all participants

TIME

- ◆ 10 minutes for setup and explanation of planning tool

- ◆ 10 minutes for individual planning

- ◆ 15 minutes to share action plans

- ◆ 10 minutes for debriefing

INSTRUCTIONS

1. Hand out copies of the Training Instrument 11–3: Negotiation Success Plan to all participants and ask them to take out a pen or pencil.

2. Explain that in a few minutes you will ask them to complete this planning document individually and then share their plan with a partner.

3. Walk the participants through the instrument, and explain the intent to use it as both an accountability and planning tool. Emphasize that with a written document, there is greater commitment to follow through with our plans.

4. Allow up to 10 minutes for the participants to complete the planning instrument. Participants should address a future negotiation situation or one they currently work on as a lead negotiator or a negotiation team member.

5. After 10 minutes, ask the participants to pair up (one group of three is fine if there is an uneven number of learners in the workshop).

6. Give the paired participants up to 15 minutes to share their success plans with each other, and explain that sharing them with other people also leads to greater accountability.

7. When it appears that all participant pairs have finished their negotiation success plans, begin the debriefing discussion.

DEBRIEFING

Ask for a handful of volunteer participants to share their negotiation success plans with the large group. Lead the debriefing into a discussion of the participants' reactions to the exercise, what they perceive as the value of completion of a success plan, and whether they found it helpful to take the time to think about, document, and share steps for successful negotiations. (10 minutes)

Handout 12–1

Nonverbal Communication Chart (Structured Experience 12–4)

Common Nonverbal Communication Behaviors (United States)

Behavior	Emotions Conveyed
Hands on hips	Skeptical Impatient Irritated
Leaning forward in seat	Attentive Cooperative Interested
Biting lip	Uncertain Puzzled Worried
Looking at objects (clock, door, or out the window)	Bored Preoccupied Disinterested
Lack of eye contact	*In some cultures:* Respectful Deferential *In other cultures:* Disrespectful Dishonest Intimidated
Nodding head	Interested Evaluative Agreeable
Fidgeting	Nervous Bored Uncomfortable
Smiling	Confident Cooperative Agreeable
Hands clasped behind head	Dominant Ambivalent Confident
Crossed arms or legs	Suspicious Closed Unreceptive
Touching face or clothing	Insecure Nervous Distracted

Adapted from: Stark, Peter B., and Jane Flaherty. *The Only Negotiating Guide You'll Ever Need: 101 Ways to Win Every Time in Any Situation.* New York: Broadway Books, 2003.

Handout 12–2

Common Negotiation Tactics (Structured Experience 12–9)

Page 1 (Distribute this page first)

1. Lowballing

Definition: _____

_____

_____

2. Authority Limits

Definition: _____

_____

_____

3. Sweetening the Deal

Definition: _____

_____

_____

4. Disclosure

Definition: _____

_____

_____

5. Trial Balloon

Definition: _____

_____

_____

continued on next page

Handout 12–2, continued
Common Negotiation Tactics (Structured Experience 12–9)

Page 2 (Distribute at end of structured experience)

1. Lowballing: When one side in a negotiation offers you a ridiculously low price to get you to agree to a deal before they reveal its true cost. It's the "too good to be true" scenario. Once one side knows what the other wants, they work the deal back into their favor by adding terms.

2. Authority Limits: Establishes the range of authority in decision-making up front to address the approval process, as well as who are the ultimate decision makers in a negotiation. This is related to the "Higher Authority" tactic in which a counterpart needs to consult with a key decision maker before he or she proceeds with the negotiations.

3. Sweetening the Deal: Offers something extra (an add-on) to your counterpart to reach an agreement. It can break an impasse or keep momentum going during negotiations, but be careful that what you offer is not a concession that could heavily cost your side.

4. Disclosure: Reveals a piece of information to your counterpart that he or she may perceive as insider information to build trust. It can also lead the other side to reveal information, and it helps to put each other at ease. Be careful to not disclose too much information.

5. Trial Balloon: Also called "Run It Up the Flagpole," this tactic provides a piece of information, such as price, to your counterpart to gauge his or her reaction. Based on this response, you can then adjust the information or offer. It's a good way to see how far apart or close you are to reaching a deal.

Handout 12–3

Barrier Role-Play Scenarios (Structured Experience 12–10)

Scenario A (Round 1)

Negotiation Role Choices (select one of the characters to play):

Debbie, the Chief Operating Officer at a large real estate development corporation, leads a negotiation team to work out the details of a contract with Brian, the President of ABC Construction, Inc., who won the bid to build 50 homes in a new residential housing development. Although negotiations have started well, Debbie feels uncomfortable around Jeff, the construction foreman on this particular project. Jeff is part of Brian's negotiation team, and he has made occasional comments during meetings that make Debbie feel as though he does not respect her knowledge of the construction industry or her position at her company. She has mentioned this to Brian, but she is unsure whether she has addressed the issue with Jeff. Debbie has been hesitant to approach Jeff, as she wants the deal to be a win for both sides and would hate to have personal feelings get in the way. It is now time for the next meeting, which will focus on which companies to hire as subcontractors to handle the plumbing, electrical work, and landscaping.

1. Debbie—COO and negotiation lead for developer
2. Brian—President of ABC Construction
3. Jeff—Foreman for ABC Construction

Scenario B (Round 2)

Negotiation Role Choices (select one of the characters to play):

Ken, a marketing director for a national clothing retail chain, works with representatives from the company's current advertising agency, Harrison Advertising, to launch a new marketing campaign that focuses on a one-day sale that will provide deep discounts for customers on all men's and women's apparel for spring. Although most people involved on both sides of the negotiation are in agreement about the campaign (how it will look and how much it will cost), Sarah, the head of finance for the retailer, has become what Ken perceives as a roadblock. She does not think the main advertising idea, "Swing into Spring," is the most effective one that will draw customers to the store. She thinks it's been done before, is not very creative, and that the advertising agency can do much better. Sarah is an important stakeholder for the marketing campaign and her support is needed to move forward, but her behavior at meetings interferes with progress. Joe, the lead advertising representative for Harrison, has mentioned to Ken that he's concerned that Sarah is a spoiler. It's almost time for the commercials about the sale, and Joe is worried he will not have enough time to produce the ads. Everyone is about to go into the next meeting about the campaign.

1. Ken—Marketing Director for retailer
2. Sarah—Head of finance for retailer
3. Joe—Advertising agency representative

continued on next page

Handout 12–3, continued

Barrier Role-Play Scenarios (Structured Experience 12–10)

Scenario C (Round 3)

Negotiation Role Choices (select one of the characters to play):

Rick, a project manager for a high-tech organization (Future, Inc.) that makes desktop publishing software, is negotiating the terms of an agreement with Translation Needed, a company that will translate the language in the software from English to a variety of other languages so users in non-English speaking countries can use the product with ease. Deadlines appear to be an obstacle in the negotiations. Cathy, the head of software development at Future, is concerned about when the translation work will be completed; the deadline seems to change as new information about the steps in the process comes to light each time the representatives in the negotiation meet. Rick and Cathy have had numerous conversations about this issue, and now it is time to discuss it with Sue, the negotiation team leader at Translation Needed. During the course of the past two meetings, it appears that Sue has presented excuses about why the deadline needs to be later. Future has had good success with this organization in the past, so they'd like to stick with Translation Needed to get the job done. It's time for their next meeting with the negotiation teams.

1. Rick—Project manager for Future, Inc.
2. Cathy—Head of software development for Future, Inc.
3. Sue—Negotiation team leader for Translation Needed

Handout 12–4

Ethics Case Study (Structured Experience 12–11: Examining Ethics)

A representative from a biomedical firm, BioMeds, Inc. negotiated the sale of the firm's new product to PharmCom, a big pharmaceutical company. The product is a cholesterol-lowering drug that in clinical trials had fewer side effects than competing products. During the negotiations, PharmCom representatives assured BioMeds that they would heavily market the drug so BioMeds could earn royalties from sales. The terms of the agreement, however, gave PharmCom the right to shelve the drug if it wanted to and move forward with a marketing campaign at its discretion. Once the sale was complete, PharmCom decided to stop marketing the drug. BioMeds later learned PharmCom never really intended to sell the drug; it was just trying to get the BioMeds product off the market because it competed with two similar products it currently sells to the public and markets to physicians. PharmCom's current products generate a significant amount of revenue, but the company's CEO wants to see those numbers go even higher as competition increases. BioMeds entered into the agreement confident that it was a win for both them and PharmCom. The firm invested a considerable amount of time and resources to investigate pharmaceutical companies to negotiate with and sell the drug to, and PharmCom came out on top with regard to reputation. In light of the new information about the lack of marketing for the drug, BioMeds is now consulting with its attorneys to see if a lawsuit against PharmCom is in order.

Adapted from: Shell, G. Richard. *Bargaining for Advantage: Negotiation Strategies for Reasonable People.* New York: Penguin Group, 2006.

Using the Online Materials

Open the webpage www.ASTD.org/NegotiationSkillsTraining in your web browser.

DOWNLOADS

Content of the Website

The website that accompanies this workbook on negotiation skills training contains three types of files. All of the files can be used on a variety of computer platforms.

- **Adobe .pdf documents.** These include handouts, assessments, training instruments, and training tools.

- **Microsoft Word documents.** These text files can be edited to suit the specific circumstances of organizations and to fit the precise needs of trainers and trainees.

- **Microsoft PowerPoint presentations.** These presentations add interest and depth to many of the training activities included in the workbook.

- **Microsoft PowerPoint files of overhead transparency masters.** These files make it easy to print viewgraphs and handouts in black and white rather than use an office copier. They contain only text and line drawings; there are no images to print in grayscale.

Computer Requirements

To read or print the .pdf files on the website, Adobe Acrobat Reader software must be installed on your system. This program can be downloaded free of cost from the Adobe website, www.adobe.com.

To use or adapt the contents of the PowerPoint presentation files on the website, Microsoft PowerPoint software must be installed on your system. If you just want to view the PowerPoint documents, you must have an appropriate viewer installed on your system. Microsoft provides downloads of various viewers free of charge on its website, www.microsoft.com.

Printing From the Website

TEXT FILES

You can print the training materials using Adobe Acrobat Reader. Just open the .pdf file and print as many copies as you need. The following documents can be printed directly from the website:

- ♦ Assessment 11–1: Learning Needs-Assessment Sheet

- ♦ Assessment 11–2: Negotiation Self-Assessment

- ♦ Assessment 11–3: Needs-Assessment Discussion Form

- ♦ Assessment 11–4: Facilitator Competencies

- ♦ Assessment 11–5: Negotiation Skills Follow-Up Assessment

- ♦ Assessment 11–6: Training Evaluation

- ♦ Assessment 11–7: Nonverbal Communication Self-Assessment

- ♦ Training Instrument 11–1: Negotiation Conversation Preparation Sheet

- ♦ Training Instrument 11–2: Brainstorming Checklist

- ♦ Training Instrument 11–3: Negotiation Success Plan

- ♦ Training Instrument 11–4: Facilitation Preparation Checklist

- ♦ Handout 12–1: Nonverbal Communication Chart

- ♦ Handout 12–2: Common Negotiation Tactics

- ♦ Handout 12–3: Barrier Role-Play Scenarios

- ♦ Handout 12–4: Ethics Case Study

POWERPOINT SLIDES

You can print the presentation slides directly from the website using Microsoft PowerPoint. Just open the .ppt files and print as many copies as you need. You can also make handouts of the presentations by printing 2, 4, or 6 slides per page. These slides will be in color, with design elements embedded. Power-Point also permits you to print these in grayscale or black-and-white represen-tations. Many trainers who use personal computers to project their presenta-tions bring along viewgraphs, just in case there are glitches in the system.

Adapting the PowerPoint Slides

You can modify or otherwise customize the slides by opening and editing them in the appropriate application. You must, however, retain the denotation of the original source of the material; it is illegal to pass it off as your own work. You may indicate that a document was adapted from this workbook, written and copyrighted by Lisa J. Downs and published by ASTD. The files will open as "Read Only," so before you adapt them, save them onto your hard drive under a different filename.

Showing the PowerPoint Presentations

The following PowerPoint presentations are included on the website:

- *Types of Negotiations.ppt*

- *Core Principles of Negotiation.ppt*

- *Steps to Negotiation.ppt*

- *Investigating Interests.ppt*

- *Building Trust and Relationships.ppt*

- *Negotiation Tactics.ppt*

- *Barriers to Effective Negotiation.ppt*

- *Ethics in Negotiation.ppt*

- *Negotiation Success Factors.ppt*

The presentation is in .ppt format, which means that it automatically shows full screen when you double-click on its filename. You can also open Microsoft PowerPoint and launch it from there.

Use the space bar, the enter key, or mouse clicks to advance through a show. Press the backspace key to back up. Use the escape key to exit a presentation. If you want to blank the screen to black as the group discusses a point, press the B key. Press it again to restore the show. If you want to blank the screen to a white background, do the same with the W key. Table A-1 (on p. 194) summarizes these instructions.

We strongly recommend that trainers practice presentations before they use them in training situations. You should be confident that you can cogently expand on the points featured in the presentations and discuss the methods

Table A–1 Navigating Through a PowerPoint Presentation

KEY	POWERPOINT "SHOW" ACTION
Space bar *or* Enter *or* Mouse click	Advance through custom animations embedded in the presentation.
Backspace	Back up to the last projected element of the presentation.
Escape	Abort the presentation.
B *or* b B *or* b *(repeat)*	Blank the screen to black. Resume the presentation.
W *or* w W *or* w *(repeat)*	Blank the screen to white. Resume the presentation.

for working through them. If you want to engage your training participants fully (rather than worry about how to show the next slide), become familiar with this simple technology before you need to use it. A good practice is to insert notes into the Speaker's Notes feature of the PowerPoint program, print them out, and have them in front of you when you present the slides.

For Further Reading

Bassi, Laurie J., and Darlene Russ. *What Works: Assessment, Development, and Measurement*. Alexandria, VA: ASTD, 1997.

Benoliel, Michael, and Linda Cashdan. *The Upper Hand: Winning Strategies From World-Class Negotiators*. Avon, MA: Platinum Press, 2006.

Carliner, Saul. *Training Design Basics*. Alexandria, VA: ASTD, 2003.

Cialdini, Dr. Robert B. *Influence: The Psychology of Persuasion* (Collins Business Essentials Edition). New York: Harper Collins, 2007.

Covey, Stephen R. *The 7 Habits of Highly Effective People*. New York: Free Press, 2004.

Fisher, Roger, and Daniel Shapiro. *Beyond Reason: Using Emotions as You Negotiate*. New York: Penguin Group, 2005.

Fisher, Roger, William Ury, and Bruce Patton, eds. *Getting to Yes: Negotiating Agreement Without Giving In* (2nd edition). New York: Penguin Group, 1991.

Gosselin, Tom. *Practical Negotiating: Tools, Tactics and Techniques*. Hoboken, NJ: John Wiley and Sons, 2007.

Kemp, Jerrold E., Gary R. Morrison, and Steven M. Ross. *Designing Effective Instruction* (2nd edition). Upper Saddle River, NJ: Prentice-Hall, 1998.

Kirkpatrick, Donald L., and James D. Kirkpatrick. *Evaluating Training Programs: The Four Levels* (3rd edition). San Francisco: Berrett-Koehler Publishers, 2006.

Knowles, Malcolm S., Elwood F. Holton III, and Richard A. Swanson. *The Adult Learner* (5th edition). Houston, TX: Gulf Publishing Company, 1998.

Shell, G. Richard. *Bargaining for Advantage: Negotiation Strategies for Reasonable People*. New York: Penguin Group, 2006.

Stark, Peter B., and Jane Flaherty. *The Only Negotiating Guide You'll Ever Need: 101 Ways to Win Every Time in Any Situation*. New York: Broadway Books, 2003.

Tobey, Deborah. *Needs Assessment Basics*. Alexandria, VA: ASTD, 2005.

Ury, William. *The Power of a Positive No: How to Say No and Still Get to Yes*. New York: Bantam Books, 2007.

Watkins, Michael. *Negotiation*. Boston: Harvard Business School Press, 2003.

Yelon, Stephen L. *Powerful Principles of Instruction*. White Plains, NY: Longman Publishers USA, 1996.

Lisa J. Downs is a leadership development manager for T-Mobile USA's Integrated Customer Experience Group, where she conducts communications, leadership, and management training and serves as a coach and curriculum developer. She is also the owner of DevelopmentWise, her consulting business in Redmond, Washington. Previously, Downs served as a senior learning and organizational development specialist for The Growth Partnership, Inc., a consulting firm headquartered in St. Louis, Missouri, that specializes in the accounting industry. At The Growth Partnership, she worked as a workshop facilitator, a coach for the organization's partner development program, and a curriculum designer with an emphasis on supervisory and communications skills. She was also the manager of learning and development for Clark Nuber PS, a *Best of the Best* accounting firm in the Seattle area, where she oversaw the firm's training function and led learning initiatives throughout the company. In addition, she established the Accounting Careers Program for the Washington Society of Certified Public Accountants.

Before she moved to Washington State, Downs taught language arts courses at the high school level and earned her secondary education teaching credentials in 1996, which launched her career in learning and development, training, and curriculum design. She also worked for both commercial and public radio stations in the Quad-Cities area of Illinois and Iowa.

Downs received her Master of Science in Education with a concentration in Adult Education from Western Illinois University in 2000, and she completed her undergraduate degree in speech communications in 1991 at Augustana College in Rock Island, Illinois. She is president of the ASTD's Puget Sound chapter, as of 2008, and served as its vice president of membership for two years. She is also an active member of national ASTD, the International Society for Performance Improvement, and the Seattle chapter of SHRM.

◆